# BREWING

# BREWING

## A step-by-step guide to making beer, wine and cider

**JACK THOMPSON**

ARCTURUS

ARCTURUS

This edition published in 2011 by Arcturus Publishing Limited
26/27 Bickels Yard, 151–153 Bermondsey Street,
London SE1 3HA

ISBN: 978-1-84837-753-0
AD001680EN

Printed in Singapore

The Fell Types are digitally reproduced by Igino Marini. www.iginomarini.com

# CONTENTS

ဢ

# INTRODUCTION

꙲꙲

When you think about home-brewing, it's probably ales and lagers that come to mind. However, there's much more you can brew at home, and home-brewing extends far beyond beer – although beer is still important! Each season there's a huge variety of natural ingredients available with which you can make ciders, perries, wines, cocktails, liqueurs and infusions.

Beers are not strictly tied to certain seasons, as many of their ingredients are available all year round. However, certain types are connected with specific seasons. Historically, strong beers have been brewed for centuries during the winter months for their warming qualities, and this tradition has carried on to the present day. Winter beers are always dark, strong, warming ales which keep you cosy through the coldest months. In the summer lighter beers and cool lagers are more appropriate to the hot weather and feel of the season.

Ciders and perries come into season in autumn when apples and pears are in abundance. Once you have your fruit pulped and pressed, the recipes for these drinks are very straightforward – in fact, the only ingredient for the country-style perry recipe (page 89) is pears. Any fruit that isn't pulped, pressed, brewed and enjoyed can be stored for the coming seasons.

Throughout the year, seasonal flowers can be plucked, hedgerows can be plundered and vegetables can be dug up to create country wines, liqueurs and cocktails. There are lots of country wine recipes in this book, with advice on the best time to pick the ingredients and where you can find them.

An added bonus of making all these home-brewed treats is incorporating them into your cooking. Pages 121–131 include a range of food recipes from beer-battered haddock and chips to an amuse-bouche using home-brewed cherry wine.

Cocktails, liqueurs and infusions make up the final chapter, on pages 133–139. Included here are recipes using fruit you've picked or cider and wine you've brewed. Once you have a cupboard full of various home-brewed wines you can play around with recipes and substitute ingredients.

There are few hobbies more satisfying than home-brewing and numerous reasons to try it. Here are a few:

• Once you've bought your equipment this hobby becomes relatively inexpensive. Instead of heading to your local supermarket, you can head to your local hedgerow for supplies.

• You're in charge of what you drink. You can decide the final flavour, colour and aroma. You can keep preservatives out and decide how strong you would like your brew to be.

• You learn a new skill and can reward yourself in the best way possible when you've finished!

On the next page is a guide to brewing, followed by an equipment and ingredients section to get you started. Recipes follow and are listed alphabetically and according to season, in this order: beer, cider, perry, mead and country wines. Each recipe advises how long the brew needs to mature after bottling, and how long it will keep after maturation before spoiling.

# HOME-BREWING GUIDE

🙢🙠

The brewing processes for beer, cider and country wines are different, but they have certain stages in common.

## BEER

The recipes in this book cover a range of beer styles for each season and the method varies according to which of the three brewing processes the recipe requires.

**Full mash brewing** is the most complex method, where malted grains are mashed before the hops are added.

**Malt extract brewing** is probably the most popular approach for beginners as it is quicker and requires less equipment. This method uses malted extracts rather than full grains and skips the mashing stage.

**Partial mash brewing** falls between the two, using a small amount of grains with most of the fermentable sugars derived from malt extracts.

### The stages of brewing beer

The recipes in this book differ depending on the brewing style. However, the main stages of brewing are:

• Mashing
• Sparging
• Boiling
• Pitching the yeast
• Fermenting the brew

Mashing is the first step, in which crushed, malted grains are steeped in hot water in a mash tun (page 16) to produce a liquid known as 'wort', pronounced 'wert'. Note that when brewing recipes instruct you to mash the grains or malts, this does not always mean that you include malted extracts that may be listed in the ingredients at that particular stage as well, so read the recipe carefully.

Mashing results in enzymes in the grains converting their starches into fermentable sugars. Different temperatures activate different enzymes which alter fermentation and thus the brewing, so always follow the temperatures given in the recipes. Take the temperature of the mash in several places to reach an average, and add hot or cold water to adjust it if need be.

After an hour, the starches in the grain should be converted into sugars, which you can check by performing a starch test (page 59). The next stage is to sparge the mash by sprinkling it with hot water to rinse the sugars from the grain. Most home brewers do this by either continuous sparging or batch sparging.

The former method most closely resembles the way that sparging is done in a commercial brewery. At home, it is usually done by placing the mash tun over a container large enough to hold the whole of the wort – the liquid from the mash and the sparging water combined. Above the mash tun, position a bucket containing the sparging water at the correct temperature, with a tap and a hose with a shower head.

Before starting the sparging water flowing, open the tap on the mash tun and collect 1–2 litres of wort. Pour it slowly back into the mash tun, taking care not to disturb the grain. Repeat three or four times or until the wort is quite clear. This process, called the *vorlauf*, helps to settle the bed of grain so that it acts as a filter when the mash is drained.

Next, slowly open the tap on the sparging bucket and set the tap on the mash tun to run at the same volume; the sparging water should rise no higher than the grain bed. Move the sprinkler head slowly over the grain bed to rinse out as much sugar as possible, taking care not to disturb the grain.

To perform batch sparging, drain the wort completely after using the *vorlauf* process, then fill the mash tun with the sparging water. Stir the grain bed then allow it to settle for 10 minutes. Drain off the sparge water, again after using the *vorlauf* process.

The wort must then be boiled to sterilize it, deactivate the enzymes and remove some of the proteins, and also to incorporate the hops into the brew. These are often added in stages, the earlier ones to give the bitter quality and the later ones to add aroma and flavour. At the end of the boil, the wort must be cooled quickly – standing the vessel in a sink of cold water is the best way. The wort is then decanted into a fermenting vessel, leaving the hops behind; you can also use a syphon to achieve this process, known as 'racking off'. Yeast is added, or 'pitched', an airlock is fitted and the brew is left to ferment, sometimes racked off to a secondary fermenter after the first few days. When fermentation has finished, most recipes call for 'bulk priming' with sugar to increase carbonation before the beer is syphoned off into bottles.

## CIDER

Cider is made from the fermented juice of apples, while perry comes from pears. These drinks are made by extracting the juice from the fruit by pulping and pressing, and then adding sugar and yeast. The drink is then left to ferment prior to bottling.

## WINE

Generally, country wines are made by boiling and pressing flowers, fruits and vegetables to extract flavour, adding yeast and sugar, straining the liquid and finally leaving to ferment prior to bottling.

# PART 1

# EQUIPMENT

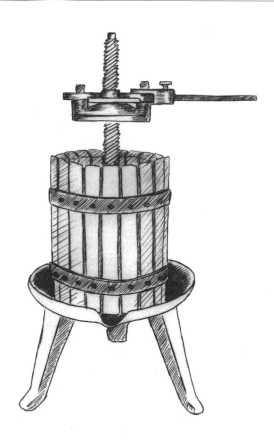

# EQUIPMENT

Home-brewing is a great hobby that requires time, skill, patience, and a lot of kit! Depending on what type of beverage you're making, you'll use different pieces of equipment. Most of the following can be bought from local home-brew supply shops or online, or even made, depending on how ambitious you are. Equipment is listed alphabetically; the accompanying illustrations are within or directly after the entry.

### AIRLOCK

The airlock does three things. First, it allows carbon dioxide to escape during fermentation. Secondly, it stops air from entering the fermentation vessel – this is essential as air could contaminate the liquid. Thirdly, it allows you to monitor how hard the yeast is working by watching how vigorously the brew is bubbling. When you are making wine, an airlock also stops fruit flies or bacteria from entering and contaminating the brew. As well as an airlock you will need a rubber stopper to seal the fermenting vessel.

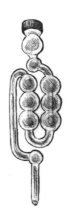

### BOTTLES

Purchase bottles that look strong and are heavy. Avoid those that come with screw tops as they will not be able to handle the pressure of bottle-conditioned beer.

Bottles made from brown glass are recommended for storing beer in particular. Brown glass prevents sunlight and fluorescent light from affecting the hop compounds, a process known as photochemistry. Remember to check the bottles for any damage before you buy them as they cannot be used if there are any imperfections. Green bottles can also be used, but they do not protect the contents as well as brown bottles. Clear bottles are good for white and light-coloured wines and dark bottles are best for darker wines or ports as they will lose their colour in a clear bottle.

### BREWING SPOON

A brewing spoon is essential as there is a lot of stirring to be done. It needs to be minimum 45 cm in length and made from plastic or stainless steel.

### BUCKET

A food-grade bucket with a lid is a useful container to have on standby during the brewing process, as it is good for mixing ingredients in. Some recipes for country wines use buckets before the liquid is transferred to another fermenting vessel or demijohn. Apples and pears could also be pulped in a bucket, in the absence of sophisticated kit.

## CARBOY

Carboys are glass containers similar to demijohns (see below). They contain 19–23 litres of liquid.

## CORKS

You will need to purchase a large quantity of corks at the same time as buying bottles – straight corks are the best.

## DEMIJOHN

A demijohn is made of glass and is easy to sanitize. One that can hold up to 5 litres should be adequate for your needs. This vessel is used for fermentation – often you'll use one as your 'primary fermenter' and then another as your 'secondary'. A demijohn can also be used when a recipe mentions a 'fermentation jar'.

## FERMENTING VESSEL

This is required for beer brewing. The type of vessel you need will depend on the type of brewing you're doing – malt extract, partial mash or full mash. For a malt extract brew you'll need a vessel with a capacity of 15 litres minimum. A 27–33 litre bin made from food-grade plastic would be ideal.

Finding one with graduated volume markings, a tap, a screw top or snap-on lid and handles will make home-browing easier and more enjoyable. Depending on a recipe's method, you may need to fit an airlock to your fermenting bin, so a lid with a hole for an airlock would also be good.

## FILTER BAG

A bag made from coarse material, or a piece of muslin, will be needed to strain flowers or fruit through. This process ensures that every last drop of juice is extracted from the pulp.

## FUNNEL

A large funnel is useful for transferring liquid in the recipes that use demijohns or carboys. These are easily available and inexpensive.

## GLOVES

Pulping and pressing fruit can be a messy task so wear medium-weight rubber household gloves.

## HYDROMETER

A hydrometer is a tool used to measure the SG (specific gravity) of your brew. In other words, it tells you the ratio of the density of the liquid to the density of water.

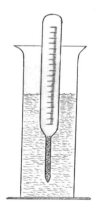

When you start brewing beer, for example, the wort contains high quantities of sugar which increases the density. The reading on the hydrometer at this stage is called the OG (original gravity). As the sugar turns to alcohol the density decreases. The final reading, taken when the fermentation has ceased, is called the FG (final gravity). With this information you can calculate the alcohol content of your brew. Your FG subtracted from your OG and multiplied by 131 gives you the ABV % (alcohol by volume). If you want to check the density, test a sample of the wort. Use a sanitized syphon to transfer the sample to a hydrometer jar – minimizing the risk of contamination is paramount.

**INSULATED MASH TUN**

For a partial mash or full mash recipe an insulated mash tun or water boiler is required. These are available from your local home-brew stores or online. If you don't want to buy one, a large coolbox, for example, can be used instead, provided it can withstand temperatures of 85°C (185°F). You'll need to customize it by adding a tap

to the box and fitting extra insulation. To use, preheat the tun with boiling hot water, closing the lid and swirling the water around. While it heats up, boil another kettle full of water and then empty the tun and refill with the water from the kettle. Repeat for a second time and the tun should maintain a good temperature. Once it is at the correct temperature you can add the grains. The mash tun is used for the mashing of the grains in hot water, causing the enzymes to convert the starches into sugars.

**KETTLE**

There is a lot of water to be boiled in home-brewing.

A saucepan or large capacity water boiler can be used for this, but an ordinary kettle works if you need a small quantity boiled quickly.

## MATERIAL

A lot of the mead and wine recipes ask you to cover a bowl or pan containing the fruit, flowers or vegetables overnight. Each recipe differs, but generally a clean tea towel or other loose-weave material is good for this as it keeps insects out but allows the liquid to breathe. Keep the bowl or pan in a cool area.

## SAUCEPAN

Some recipes ask you to use cool, pre-boiled water and this is where the saucepan comes in. The water can be boiled and then stored in the saucepan until needed. A lot of the country wine recipes require the fruit or vegetables to be boiled to begin the process of extracting the flavour. An ordinary

household saucepan with a large capacity is ideal.

## SPARGE BAG

A sparge bag, also known as a 'grain bag', contains the crushed grains. It is usually steeped in hot water, which releases the flavour and aroma of the grains.

## SPARGER

A sparger is required if you're doing a partial or full mash. Sparging rinses the fermentable sugars from the grains by spraying a large quantity of hot water through a hose with a fine shower head. An insulated bin with a tap at the bottom works well, with a capacity of around 19 litres. The picture on the next page shows a homemade sparger, with a plank of wood across the boiler and a hose attached.

## SYPHON TUBE

A syphon tube transfers liquid from one container to another, leaving the unwanted elements such as the sediment behind. If a recipe asks you to 'rack' it is referring to the syphoning process.

## THERMOMETER

Thermometers are an essential tool to have on hand during the brewing process. Certain steps during brewing take place at specific temperatures, such as adding ingredients, so you need to be able to monitor the temperature of your brew.

## WATER BOILER

For a partial or full mash you'll need a large container with a minimum capacity of 19 litres – 27 litres is ideal.

If possible, a boiler with a tap and heating element would be best, as this allows you to set and maintain the temperature. It should have a 'false bottom' made of fine mesh stainless steel just above the tap. This will stop the grains from gathering around the heating element or blocking the tap. A large pot heated on a stove can suffice if your budget is restricted, though it would need to be able to hold a lot of liquid.

## WINE AND CIDER PRESS

A press is used to extract the juice from fruit. If you're making wine, the fruit can easily be pressed at home.

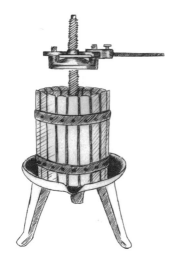

Fill a bucket with fruit or vegetables and, using an implement such as a potato masher, you can squash the produce yourself. However, to ensure the maximum amount of juice is extracted, a proper press will do the job well, and you'll get considerably less messy in the process!

For cider and perry making, you'll need to get the fruit pulped prior to pressing. It is usually possible to get this done at cider or wine centres or local breweries.

## WINE RACK

Once you have bottled your brew you'll need to store it properly. A wine rack needs to be positioned in an area with a constant temperature of 9–15°C (48–59°F) and out of direct sunlight. Beers and ciders should also be stored this way.

# CLEANING AND SANITIZING
෮෮

The most important aspect of the home-brewing process is the cleaning and sanitizing of the equipment we use and the area we work in. This may seem surprising, but it's the bacteria and micro-organisms all around you, on every surface and on your hands, that can infiltrate your brew and ruin it.

To properly protect from contamination, you need to clean and sanitize everything your brew comes into contact with. Although cleaning won't completely kill off the bacteria and micro-organisms, it will reduce their effect to a harmless level.

First, a bit of elbow grease and some unscented washing-up liquid will remove dust, dirt, scum and other visible contaminants. Thoroughly rinse after.

Secondly, sanitizing will get rid of invisible contaminants, the bacteria and micro-organisms that cling on despite your vigorous scrubbing. For this, you need chemicals. The easiest thing to use is a bleach solution – 3 tablespoons of bleach to 5 litres of water. You'll find a range of purpose-made sanitizers in your local home-brew store. The ones to look out for contain iodine, chlorine, acid or oxygen as the main active ingredient.

Rinse the equipment thoroughly after using chemicals as any traces that remain can impart flavours and affect the brew. Be sure to follow all manufacturers' instructions on the product labels as sometimes these chemicals can be rather volatile.

In wine making, Campden tablets are often used – you'll see them popping up frequently in ingredients lists throughout this book. The active ingredient is potassium metabisulphite and you can also buy it under this name. Fourteen crushed Campden tablets dissolved in 4 litres of water makes an excellent sanitizing solution for use in wine making.

Sterilizing is the third part of your attack strategy and this occurs naturally when your brew is subjected to high temperatures. Micro-organisms just love the warmth and sweetness of the brew but they will not survive the heat.

Once your wort cools, the danger of contamination returns. Your brew can be affected by airborne, waterborne and human-borne germs, so keep an eye on it and safeguard it from bacterial opportunists.

There are some steps you can take to minimize the risk of contamination.
• Keep your work area clean and dust-free.
• Every cough or sneeze during the process is a potential contaminant, so try to move well away.
• Keep all family pets in an area of the house far away from the brew.
• Once you've finished with the equipment, clean, rinse, dry and store somewhere dry and mildew-free.

# INGREDIENTS

There are many ingredients involved in the flavouring and colouring of an alcoholic beverage. Besides the four main ingredients in beer – malted barley, hops, yeast and water – there are additional ingredients, known as adjuncts. A few examples of these are unmalted or roasted barley, wheat, rice, oak chips and flaked oats.

In brewing, malts usually refer to malted barley or other grains that have gone through the malting process. There is a range of malts to choose from: some are referred to as base malts, others as speciality. Malts contribute flavour, body and character to beer and can be purchased as grain, crushed grain or malt extract.

Hops (*Humulus lupulus*) are used in beer brewing for their natural preservatives, flavouring and aroma. They are known by four types: bittering, flavouring, aroma and finishing. You'll notice on some recipes that you add hops at different stages in the brewing process. This is because the flavour and aroma of some hops can be released and lost if boiled for too long, so it takes careful timing to capture the best from your ingredients.

Mead, wine, cider and perry also contain ingredients beyond fruit and sugar. Citric acid, tartaric acid and acid blend are common ingredients in the wine recipes as they compensate for the lack of acid in the fruit. Adding acid gives an authentic wine taste.

Some of the ingredients you will need for the recipes in this book are as follows.

## AMBER MALT
Used in brown porters.
Biscuit, bitter and toasted
flavours.

## BLACK MALT
Smoky, rich flavours. Dark in
colour, ideal in dark beers
such as stouts or porters.

## BROWN MALT
A darker form of pale malt.
Nutty, caramel and smoky
flavours.

## CAMPDEN TABLETS
A sulphur-based product used
to kill bacteria.

## CARAMALT
An aroma hop with caramel
and nutty flavours, used in
light beers.

## CASCADE HOPS
Flowery, spicy and citrus-like
flavours. Moderate bitterness.
Can be used in most ales,
lagers, barley wines and
porters.

## CHALLENGER HOPS
Crisp and fruity flavours.
Aroma and bittering qualities.

## CHINOOK HOPS
Piney, herbal and spicy
flavours, with hints of
grapefruit.

## CHOCOLATE MALT
Used in porters, dark lagers
and sweet stouts. Smooth,
mocha and chocolate
flavours.

## CRYSTAL MALT
Very sweet, toffee, nut and
biscuit flavours. Used in pale
ales and bitters.

## FLAKED OATS
These give a creamy finish
and are usually found in
stout recipes.

## FUGGLES HOPS

Famous English aroma hop. Earthy, fruit and sweet flavours, used in pale ales, bitters and browns.

## GOLDINGS HOPS

Traditional English aroma hop. Smooth, sweet and gently hoppy flavours ideal in English or Scottish ales. Sometimes listed as 'Kent Goldings'.

## GYPSUM

A soft mineral used to add hardness to water.

## HALLERTAUER HOPS

Named after the Hallertau district in Bavaria. Used in pale German lagers, bocks, wheat beers or pilsners. Mild spicy flavour and pleasant aroma.

## IRISH MOSS

A clarifying agent added when the wort is boiling.

## LOVIBOND SCALE

In a few recipes in this book you'll see a number and the letter 'L' after the name of a malt. For example, on the recipe for English Mild on page 59, you'll find:

230 g crystal malt 50–60 L
170 g crystal malt 135–165 L

The L is referring to the depth of colour of the malt. The higher the number, the deeper the colour. 50–60 L means the colour will be amber and the flavour will be caramel. A lower number would translate as a minimal colour and slight caramel flavour. The second quantity of crystal malt above is 135–165 L, which means the colour is a deep red and the caramel flavour is rich. At the end of the scale is black patent malt 500 L which is the darkest malt, used in stouts and porters. This scale was devised by British brewer Joseph Lovibond in the 18th century.

## MUNICH MALT

Deep red with amber tones and malty flavours. Ideal in bocks or marzenbiers.

## NORTHERN BREWER HOPS

Mild bitterness, good for bittering stouts and porters. Wood and mint notes.

## PALE ALE MALT

A base malt which is light in colour, used in most British ales.

## PECTIN ENZYME

Also known as Pectolase. It clears the brew by removing pectin (residual fruit starch) from country wines, ciders and perries.

## PILSNER MALT

A base malt which is used in continental lagers. Sweet flavours.

## SAAZ HOPS

Well-known aroma hop. Best for pilsners and European lagers.

## STERLING HOPS

Herbal, spicy and citrus flavours. Perfect in ales, pilsners and lagers.

## VIENNA MALT

A base malt with subtle grainy flavours and caramel aroma.

## WHEAT

Unmalted wheat is added to aid head retention and add body.

## WILLAMETTE HOPS

Fragrant, spicy and woody aroma. Excellent in ales and lagers.

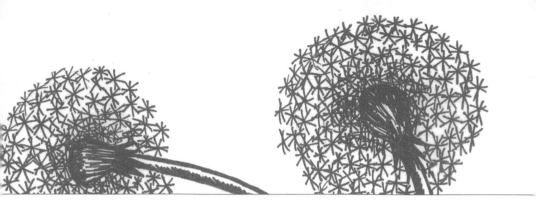

# PART 2

# SPRING

# BREWING IN SPRING

ॐ

As the winter chill loses its bite and the days get longer and brighter, the home-brewer can look forward to a busy season ahead. However, before you start foraging and harvesting, it is vitally important to ensure your equipment is properly sanitized before use. All work surfaces, demijohns, fermenting vessels, buckets, syphon tubing, even your brewing spoon, need to be thoroughly cleaned to tackle any bacteria and micro-organisms that have had a chance to build up. Carefully inspect all the bottles you intend to use once you've made your brew, and discard any that are damaged in any way. See pages 20–21 for more information on the cleaning and sanitizing of your equipment.

## BEER

Beers and ales vary from light golden colours through to deep brown and black. The darker beers are most strongly associated with the winter months and lighter beers seem more appropriate to the weather and typical food of the spring season.

Belgian Trappist white beer (page 32) and Bière de Garde (page 33) are excellent beers for the spring season as they are light and very carbonated, perfect refreshing drinks after a long day. There are certain ales that are brewed specially for the springtime. Bock (page 34) originated in 14th-century Einbeck, Germany, and the story goes that it was brewed by Roman Catholic monks to sustain them through Lent, when they would be fasting.

Bohemian pilsner (page 35) is a pale lager with a relatively low alcohol content. The finished beverage should be a golden colour and have a hoppy aroma.

There are several variations on the 'bock' style and Eisbock (page 36) is a popular one. As a result of the freeze distilling technique used when brewing Eisbock, the resulting drink is high in alcohol concentration and has a pleasant ruby appearance.

Irish stout (page 37) is brewed for the spring because of its links to the annual St Patrick's Day holiday in Ireland on 17 March. While Guinness is the consumers' choice for this festival, the home-brewer can enjoy stout on another level, taking personal pride in their drink made from scratch. Stout should be dark and thick, and the barley and hop flavours should be strong.

Spruce beer (page 38) has an interesting cola-like taste.

The outer tips on spruce trees are used to brew this beer – be sure to pick tips that are soft and bright green, as they will hold the most flavour.

## CIDER AND PERRY

With the weather brightening up, lazy afternoons in the sun don't feel a million miles away, and what better to pair them with than an ice-cold home-brewed cider or perry. The savvy brewer will have picked and stored apples and pears from last autumn's harvest in preparation for this year's cider and perry production. Cider and perry are made in much the same way and after storing the apples and pears through the winter, now is the time to get them pulped and pressed. It is possible to get this done at breweries but arguably it could be more fun to either buy a cider press kit or build your own cider press. It is important to sort through your apples and pears and discard any that are bruised or showing signs of decay before you pulp them. A golden semi-dry perry (page 40) or a classic South West England scrumpy (page 39) are excellent drinks to get you in the mood for the coming summer season.

## MEAD AND COUNTRY WINE

Now is a good time to go foraging and pick some wild ingredients for delicious country wines. Whether you grow your own produce or plunder local hedgerows, there is a wide variety of ingredients available in this season.

Dandelions (*Taraxacum officinalis*) bloom from about April and can be picked anywhere grassy in temperate regions. Be careful to avoid the stalks when picking the flowers as they contain a bitter 'milk' which can affect the taste of the finished drink. The petals can be boiled with restorative ingredients to make a healthy mead (see pages 41–42). Alternatively, a refreshing wine (page 45) can be produced with dandelion petals, sultanas, sugar and tea.

A twist on this drink is dandelion and burdock beer (page 46), a traditional British drink – actually a wine, in spite of its name – that has been consumed in this country since the 13th century. Burdock roots are best harvested after the first frost in their first year, or in the spring in their second year. Depending on when you dig them, you may need to store them until required. To keep burdock in optimum condition, lightly scrub the root to remove any soil and then trim off the very top of the root. If the root appears black or feels soft, chop it up into small pieces and immerse in cold water to prevent oxidation. Wrap the burdock in a wet paper towel and place inside a plastic bag. Store the bag in the fridge for a few months, or in the freezer for up to a year.

Oak leaves are in abundance in spring, and you can start picking these to brew wines and meads. The recipe for oak leaf mead is on page 43 and the recipe for wine is on page 51. Coltsfoot (*Tussilago farfara*) flowers are similar in appearance to dandelions and start to pop up in March. Interestingly, smoking the dried leaves of coltsfoot is an ancient remedy for asthma and lung ailments, so perhaps this plant is worth brewing for its health benefits as well as for enjoyment (see page 44).

Elderflowers (*Sambucus nigra*) come into bloom towards the end of May and they can be found in parks and wooded areas. The heads of elderflowers make a refreshing wine with a delightful fragrance. Included in this section are two wonderful recipes using elderflowers (see pages 47 and 48).

The flowers of gorse (*Ulex europaeus*) are in bloom from March to June and can usually be found in rough, overgrown areas and on the edges of heaths. These flowers have a distinctive scent like that of coconut which is, strangely, obvious to some but completely undetectable to others. See the recipe on page 49. Make extra gorse wine to use in cocktails come New Year celebrations (see page 137).

Nettles are everywhere come spring so you should end up with an impressive supply. Remember to wear gloves when picking the nettles as they will sting on contact. Make sure your arms and legs are covered too. If you do get stung, a dock leaf will relieve the pain. Pick only the young tips of the nettles as they are sweet and will produce a nice flavour. See page 50 for a recipe for a beautiful nettle wine.

# BELGIAN TRAPPIST WHITE BEER

### Ingredients

680 g cane sugar

water

1 tsp lemon juice

4.5 kg pilsner malt

450 g wheat malt

115 g rice hulls

55 g Goldings hops

27 g Hallertauer hops

11 g Belgian ale yeast

135 g cane sugar, for bottle conditioning

**Mature for**: 1 month

**Drink within**: 6 months

### Method

**1** Make a syrup by heating the sugar with a small amount of water. Add the lemon juice. When the syrup turns a light yellow colour it is ready.

**2** Heat 8 litres of water to 65°C (149°F) and add to an insulated mash tun. Add the pilsner malt, wheat malt and rice hulls to a sparge bag and mash for 90 minutes. Sparge with 8 litres of water at 75°C (167°F).

**3** Add the sugar syrup, 42 g Goldings hops and 14 g Hallertauer hops and boil for 90 minutes.

**4** Eighty-five minutes in to the boil, add the remaining hops.

**5** Chill the wort and strain into a fermenter. Top up with water to 23 litres.

**6** Pitch the yeast at 21°C (70°F) and leave to ferment for 7 days.

**7** After 7 days, transfer to a secondary fermenter for 2 weeks.

**8** Bulk prime with 135 g of cane sugar prior to bottling.

---

### TRAPPIST TIPPLE

Trappist beers get their name from trappist monks, a Roman Catholic religious order of contemplative monks who originally brewed it.

# BIÈRE DE GARDE

ཙཙ

## Ingredients

5.5 kg Vienna malt

350 g Belgian aromatic malt

250 g white wheat malt

170 g Belgian Special B malt

water

28 g Mount Hood hops

28 g Spalter hops

28 g Sterling hops

200 g brown sugar

11 g Bière de Garde yeast

100 g brown sugar, for bottle conditioning

**Mature for:** 1 month

**Drink within:** 6 months

## Method

**1** Combine the grains and mash at 63°C (145°F) for 30 minutes.

**2** Increase the temperature to 66°C (150°F). Stand for 40 minutes.

**3** Mash out at 75.5°C (167.9°F) for ten minutes and sparge.

**4** Mash the grains for 60 minutes in 8 litres of water heated to 75°C (167°F).

**5** Heat 12 litres of water to 75°C (167°F) and rinse through the grains.

**6** Bring the liquid to a boil and add the Mount Hood hops. Boil for 60 minutes.

**7** After 45 minutes, add the Spalter hops and 14 g Sterling.

**8** At 55 minutes, add the remainder of the hops and 200 g brown sugar.

**9** After 60 minutes, turn off the heat. Take out the hops and put in a fermenting vessel. Top up the volume to 19 litres.

**10** When the temperature is at 21°C (70°F), pitch the yeast.

**11** Ferment for 2 weeks at 21°C (70°F) and then transfer to a secondary fermenter at the same temperature for a further 3 weeks.

**12** Bulk prime with 100 g brown sugar prior to bottling.

# BOCK

Bocks were first brewed in 14th-century Germany and were traditionally drunk on special occasions such as Easter or Lent.

## Ingredients

225 g aromatic malt
225 g dextrine malt
225 g caramel malt 10 L water
3.25 kg pale liquid malt extract
56 g Cascade hops
1 tsp Irish moss
44 g Chinook hops
11 g Bock lager yeast
90 g cane sugar, for bottle
   conditioning
**Mature for**: 6 weeks
**Drink within**: 6 months

## Method

**1** Add the grains to 8 litres of water. Slowly increase the temperature to 75°C (167°F).
**2** Using a strainer, remove the grains and discard them.
**3** Bring the liquid to the boil and then add the pale liquid malt extract and Cascade hops.
**4** Boil for 60 minutes. Thirty minutes in add the Irish moss and 30 g Chinook hops.
**5** When the 60 minutes is up, transfer hops to a fermenting container. Fill up to 19 litres.
**6** Pitch yeast at 21°C (70°F) and ferment for three days.
**7** Rack off to a secondary fermenter and add the remaining 14 g Chinook hops.
**8** Ferment for 3 weeks at 16°C (60°F).
**9** Bulk prime with 90 g cane sugar prior to bottling.

### BOCKTOBERFEST!

In Texas, USA, an annual event called Bocktoberfest is held to celebrate the history of bock beers.

# BOHEMIAN PILSNER

## Ingredients

225 g crystal malt 20 L
450 g Pilsner malt
225 g dextrine malt
water
3 kg light liquid malt extract
112 g Sterling hops
1 tsp Irish moss
11 g pilsner yeast
110 g cane sugar for bottle
  conditioning
**Mature for:** 3–4 weeks
**Drink within:** 6 months

## Method

**1** Steep the malts in 8 litres of water at 65°C (149°F) for 30 minutes.
**2** Using a strainer, remove the grain from the hot water and discard.
**3** Remove the pot from the heat and add 50 g light liquid malt extract.
**4** Bring the water to the boil and add 56 g hops and the Irish moss. Boil for 45 minutes.

**5** Fifteen minutes into this boil, add 28 g hops.
**6** Thirty minutes into this boil, add the last of the hops.
**7** In the last few minutes of the boil, add the remaining light liquid malt extract and stir. Leave for 10 minutes.
**8** Fill your fermenter with 8 litres of cold water.
**9** Strain the hot wort into the fermenter and make up the volume to 19 litres.
**10** When the temperature of the beer is below 24°C (75°F) pitch the yeast and ferment at 10–15°C (50–59°F). Store for 4 weeks.
**11** Bulk prime with 110 g of cane sugar before bottling.

---

### CZECH MATE

The pilsner style of beer was developed at Plzen in the Czech Republic and was first served on 11 November 1842.

---

35

# EISBOCK

తంఠ

## Ingredients

700 g caraMunich malt

water

3.5 kg liquid amber malt extract

1.5 kg liquid dark malt extract

56 g Hallertauer hops

1 tsp Irish moss

11 g Bock lager yeast

60 g cane sugar, for bottle
  conditioning

**Mature for:** 6 weeks

**Drink within:** 6 months

## Method

**1** Put the grains in a sparge bag and steep in 8 litres of water heated to 65°C/149°F. Leave for 45 minutes.

**2** Discard the grains and bring the liquid to the boil.

**3** Add the malt extracts and 28 g Hallertauer hops. Boil for 60 minutes.

**4** Forty-five minutes in to the boil, add the remaining 28 g hops and the Irish moss.

**5** After 60 minutes, turn off the heat. Take out the hops and transfer to a fermenting vessel. Top up the vessel with water to 19 litres.

**6** When the temperature is at 21°C (70°F), pitch the yeast.

**7** Ferment for 3 days and then rack off to a secondary fermenting vessel.

**8** Ferment for 3 weeks at 16°C (61°F).

**9** Transfer to an open-topped vessel that will fit in your freezer. Freeze until a slushy consistency is reached. Set a strainer over a second open-topped container and pour in the frozen beer. You should obtain 14 litres of concentrated beer – if there is less, let the icy slush remaining in the strainer thaw so that more drips through. Discard the ice.

**10** Bulk prime with 60 g cane sugar prior to bottling.

# IRISH STOUT
ᔑᔑ

## Ingredients

3 kg pilsner malt

water

250 g wheat malt

170 g black patent malt

170 g chocolate malt

1 kg flaked barley

500 g roasted barley

43 g Northern Brewer hops

11 g ale yeast

72 g cane sugar, for bottle
   conditioning

**Mature for:** 6 weeks

**Drink within:** 6 months

## Method

**1** Two days before brew day,
make a sour mash. Add 225 g
pilsner malt to 1 litre of water
at 55°C (131°F). Leave to sour
for two days.

**2** On brew day, mash the
remaining malts and adjuncts
with 11 litres of water at 65°C
(149°F) for 90 minutes.

**3** Combine with the sour mash.

**4** Increase the temperature to
75°C (167°F) for 10 minutes.

**5** Sparge with 18 litres of
water at 75°C (167°F),
collecting 20–23 litres of wort.

**6** Add 28 g hops to the wort
and boil. After 30 minutes,
add the remainder of the hops
and allow to boil for another
30 minutes.

**7** Cool the wort to 20°C (68°F)
and pitch the yeast.

**8** After one week in the
primary fermenter, rack off to
a secondary fermenter.

**9** Bulk prime with 72 g cane
sugar. You want the finished
consistency to be creamy,
not fizzy.

# SPRUCE BEER

Spruce beer is a classic country beverage. The tips of spruce foliage produce interesting citrus and cola-like flavours.

## Ingredients
22.5 litres water
115 g dried, bruised root ginger
56 g Fuggles hops
500 g spruce fir – the tips (light green colour)
3.5 litres molasses
11 g brewer's yeast
**Mature for:** 5 days
**Drink within:** 6 months.

## Method
**1** Combine the water, root ginger, hops and twigs in a large pan.
**2** Boil this mixture until the hops sink to the bottom.
**3** Strain into a large container and add the molasses. Once the mixture has cooled to room temperature, add the yeast, then cover and leave for 48 hours.
**4** Bottle, cap and store in a warm place (21–24°C/70–75°F) for five days before drinking.

### SPRUCE TIP
Light or dark treacle is a good substitute for molasses if you aren't able to obtain it easily.

### VASHE ZDOROVIE!
Home-brewers in Russia add horseradish to their version of spruce beer.

# SCRUMPY CIDER

This recipe makes a strong, dry cider.

## Ingredients

3.6 kg apples, skin on
10 litres water
28 g root ginger
juice of 4 lemons
1 kg white sugar
**Mature for:** 2 months
**Drink within:** 1 year

*Note – do not use any metallic utensils*

## Method

**1** Roughly chop up the apples and cover with 9 litres of boiling water.
**2** Leave the mixture for two weeks. Crush the apples every now and then. Ensure that no mould forms during this time.
**3** Boil a litre of water.
**4** Strain the liquid from the apples and add to it the ginger, lemon juice and sugar.
**5** Add the boiled litre of water and leave to stand again for two weeks. Check for scum rising to the surface of the mixture and skim it off.
**6** Strain into resealable bottles. Screw the lids to a point where they are not completely tight – as if one more turn would seal them.
**7** Five weeks later, tighten the lids all the way and store for two months in a cool, dark and dry area.

### SCRUMPIN' FOR APPLES

The word 'scrumpy' derives from the old dialect word 'scrimp', which means 'withered apple'.

# GOLDEN PERRY

This recipe makes a delicious golden semi-dry perry.

## Ingredients
18 litres pear juice
1.8 kg white sugar
900 kg light brown sugar
5 tsp malic acid
3 tsp tartaric acid
2 tsp acid blend
1.5 tsp citric acid
1 tsp tannin
10 g champagne yeast
water
**Mature for:** 6 months
**Drink within:** 1 year

## Method
**1** Heat 3.7 litres pear squeezings with the sugars, acids and tannin until they are dissolved.
**2** Reconstitute the dried yeast in some warm water (32° 37°C/90–99°F).

**3** Add the remaining pear juice to the mixture and transfer to a 23 litre demijohn. Fit a venting tube to the container to allow any excess foam to escape and pitch the yeast.
**4** Monitor the liquid level and top up with pear juice as required.
**5** Leave to ferment for a month and then rack off to a secondary demijohn, top up with some fresh pear juice and bottle.

### GOLDEN WONDER
Golden perry will taste best if left to mature for six months.

# DANDELION MEAD

Mead is neither a beer, cider, or wine, but it is too good to leave out! Pick your dandelions in spring and make a refreshing mead or wine.

### Ingredients
250 g dandelion petals
3 cm piece of root ginger, bruised
juice and zest of 1 lemon
4.5 litres unchlorinated water
500 g honey
500 g demerara sugar
25 g cream of tartar
2 tsp yeast nutrient
2.5 g champagne yeast
**Mature for:** 1 year
**Drink within:** 1 year

### Method
1 Place the dandelions, ginger, lemon juice and zest in a large pot, add enough water to cover and bring to the boil.
2 Simmer for 10 minutes.
3 Add the honey and sugar. Once the sugar has dissolved, turn off the heat and top up the volume to 4.5 litres.
4 Add the cream of tartar. Let the mixture cool slightly and then strain.
5 Check the temperature and once it is at 37°C (99°F) add the yeast nutrient and yeast.
6 Cover with kitchen foil and store in a warm area.
7 Strain into a secondary fermenting bin and fit an airlock. The airlock should start bubbling and foam will form on the top of the liquid.
8 After 30 days, or when the sediment is 2–3 cm deep, rack off into another fermenting vessel and top up with water. Try to expose to as little oxygen as possible. The intense bubbling in the airlock should have subsided by now.

**9** Check the mead daily and repeat the racking process as the sediment builds up again. Top up as necessary.

**10** When the bubbling has ceased entirely the fermentation is complete.
**11** Bottle and leave to mature for one year.

### DANDELION DETOX

In traditional Chinese medicine, dandelions are used to aid liver detoxification as they are known to be a natural diuretic.

### DANDELION DATA

• Dandelion flowers open in the morning and close at night.
• Dandelion roots may be roasted and used as a coffee substitute.

# OAK LEAF MEAD

ଚ୍ଚ

## Ingredients

withered oak leaves   enough
   to fill a 5-litre pot
5 litres unchlorinated water
5 cm piece of root ginger,
   bruised
500 g chopped raisins
4 kg honey
2.5 g wine yeast
**Mature for:** 1 year
**Drink within:** 1 year

## Method

**1** Place the oak leaves in a
bucket and pour over 5 litres
of boiling water.
**2** Cover the bucket and leave
for 4–5 days.
**3** Strain through a muslin into
a large container.
**4** Add the ginger and raisins
to the oak leaf liquid and boil.
**5** Add the honey a little at a
time and stir the mixture until
it dissolves.
**6** Add the yeast.
**7** Take the mixture off the heat

and extract the ginger.
**8** Cover the mixture with some
clean aluminium foil and
allow to cool to 37°C (99°F).
**9** Transfer to a demijohn, top
up with water, and fit a bung
and an airlock.
**10** Place in a cool, dark place
and check the airlock each
day, monitoring that the mead
is bubbling vigorously at first.
**11** After 30 days, or when the
sediment is 2–3 cm deep, rack
off into another fermenting
vessel and top up with water.
Try to expose to as little
oxygen as possible. The
intense bubbling in the airlock
should have subsided by now.
**12** Refit airlock and store.
**13** Check the mead daily and
repeat the racking process as
the sediment builds up again.
Top up as necessary.
**14** When the bubbling has
ceased entirely the
fermentation is complete.

# COLTSFOOT WINE

## Ingredients
3 litres coltsfoot flowers
4.5 litres water
juice of 2 lemons
1 kg white sugar
2.5 g wine yeast
**Mature for:** 1 month
**Drink within:** 1 year

## Method

**1** Put the coltsfoot flowers in a bucket and cover with 2 litres of boiling water. Leave them to soak for 24 hours. Press the flowers every now and then with a wooden spoon.

**2** Strain the liquid into another container and add the lemon juice.

**3** Boil the sugar in 2 litres of water and add to the mixture.

**4** When the mixture has cooled to room temperature, add the yeast. Cover the container and store.

**5** Three days later, transfer the mixture to a fermentation jar (with fitted airlock) and top up with the remaining water. Ensure the jar is closed properly. Store in a warm area with a temperature of 16–20°C (61–68°F).

**6** Once fermentation has finished, syphon off the wine into a domijohn, ensuring the sediment is left behind. Seal and store for a month.

### COLTSFOOT CURE

A herbal tea can be made from the discarded coltsfoot leaves to help soothe an irritating cough.

# DANDELION WINE

## Ingredients

3.5 litres dandelion petals

450 g sultanas, chopped

284 ml strong black tea

1 kg sugar

5 ml citric acid

4 litres boiling water

2.5 g wine yeast

1 tsp yeast nutrient

few drops of pectin enzyme

2 oranges

**Mature for:** 1 year

**Drink within:** 1 year

## Method

**1** Put the petals, sultanas, tea, sugar and citric acid into a fermenting vessel and cover with 4 litres of boiling water.

**2** Stir the mixture well to dissolve the sugar.

**3** Cover and allow the mixture to cool to a lukewarm temperature of 18°C (64°F).

**4** Uncover and add the yeast and yeast nutrient and a few drops of pectin enzyme.

**5** Grate the orange zest over the mixture.

**6** Halve the oranges and then squeeze out all the juice into the mixture.

**7** Cover again and ensure it is absolutely airtight. Store in a warm area for 8–9 days, stirring daily.

**8** Strain the solids through thick muslin.

**9** Clean the fermenting vessel and pour the strained wine back in.

**10** Cover and leave in a warm area to ferment for 5–6 days.

**11** Carefully pour the wine into a 4.5 litre jar, so the residue is left behind.

**12** Fill the jar to the base of the neck; if it doesn't reach to there top up with pre-boiled, cool water.

**13** Fit an airlock and leave to ferment.

**14** Syphon into bottles when fermentation has finished.

# DANDELION AND BURDOCK BEER

Though this is sometimes traditionally called a 'beer', it is actually a hedgerow wine flavoured with the root of the burdock.

## Ingredients
4 large burdock roots, chopped into small pieces
3 large dandelion roots, chopped into small pieces
4 litres water
900 g sugar cubes
3 oranges, cut into segments, peel on
3 lemons, cut into segments, peel on
5 g yeast
1 piece of toast
**Mature for:** 2 months
**Drink within:** 6 months

## Method
**1** Add the burdock and dandelion roots to a bucket and pour over 4 litres of water.
**2** Bring to the boil and allow to boil for 20 minutes.
**3** Add the sugar and fruit and boil for a further 10 minutes.
**4** Pour through a sieve into a fermenting bucket and allow to cool.
**5** Spread the yeast on the piece of toast and float on the surface.
**6** Leave for three days then rack into bottles.
**7** Store in a cool place for two months.

### INSECT INSIGHT
Ninety-three different kinds of insects use dandelion pollen for food.

### BURDOCK BUZZ
• Collect burdock roots as the leaves start to appear.
• Avoid burdock if you are pregnant as it has diuretic capabilities.

# ELDERFLOWER WINE

### Ingredients

600ml elderflowers

4.5 litres water

250 g raisins, chopped

zest and juice of 2 lemons

2 Campden tablets, crushed

1.4 kg sugar

1 tsp wine tannin

2.5 g wine yeast

1 tsp yeast nutrient

**Mature for:** 1 year

**Drink within:** 1 year

### Method

**1** Separate the flowers from their stalks.

**2** Press the flowers lightly in a plastic container. Meanwhile, boil the water.

**3** Add the chopped raisins and lemon zest to the petals and pour in the boiled water.

**4** Once the mixture has cooled, add 1 Campden tablet. Cover and leave to stand for three days, stirring every now and then.

**5** Add the sugar, juice from the lemons, wine tannin, yeast and yeast nutrient.

**6** Once the sugar has dissolved, strain through a muslin into a 4.5 litre fermenting demijohn and fit an airlock. Store in a warm area (20–22°C/68–72°F) for 5 days.

**7** Syphon off the liquid into another demijohn and leave to ferment.

**8** After 8 weeks the mixture will appear clear. Add 1 Campden tablet and after 24 hours bottle the wine.

---

**WITCHING HOUR**

In English folklore, the elder tree was believed to ward off malevolent forces and protect against witches.

---

# ELDERFLOWER SPARKLING WINE

## Ingredients

650 g loaf sugar

4.5 litres of water

rind and juice of 1 lemon

4 elderflower heads in full bloom

2 tbsp white wine vinegar

**Mature for:** 6–10 days

**Drink within:** 6 months

## Method

**1** Dissolve the sugar in a little warm water.

**2** Squeeze out the juice from the lemon and cut the rind into 4 pieces. Combine the juice and rind with the sugar and elderflowers in a large container.

**3** Add the vinegar and remaining water. Leave to steep for four days.

**4** Strain through muslin and bottle.

### SMELDERFLOWER

Elderflower leaves are a natural insect repellent, which is why elder shrubs are often planted around compost heaps.

### FULL BLOOM

Pick elderflowers on a dry, sunny day as this is when they're in their prime condition and holding the most nectar.

# GORSE WINE

## Ingredients

1.5 litres fresh gorse flowers
(not pressed down)
4.5 litres water
250 ml black tea
1 kg sugar
juice of 1 lemon
2.5 g wine yeast
**Mature for**: 1 month
**Drink within**: 6 months

## Method

**1** Boil the gorse flowers in 2 litres of water for 15 minutes. Sieve the resulting liquor into a demijohn.

**2** Add the tea, sugar and lemon juice. Fill with water until the quantity reaches 4.5 litres.
**3** Stir well until the sugar has dissolved.
**4** Add the yeast.
**5** Fit an airlock then leave the demijohn in a warm place. Once the density has reached 1.000 you can stop the fermentation and bottle.

### GORSE GOODNESS

• In former times, decoctions of gorse flowers were used to treat scarlet fever, jaundice and kidney stones and to treat problems with the spleen.
• Soaked gorse seeds can also be used as a flea-repellent.
• Wear a pair of thick gloves when picking these flowers.

# NETTLE WINE

### Ingredients
2 lemons
10 g root ginger, bruised
4.5 litres water
2 litres nettles
1.7 kg sugar
2.5 g wine yeast
**Mature for:** 3 months
**Drink within:** 1 year

### Method
1 Combine lemon peel, bruised root ginger, water and nettles in a pan and simmer for 50 minutes.
2 Strain and transfer to a bucket and add the sugar, stirring until it dissolves.
3 Add more water to bring the volume back up to 4.5 litres.
4 When the temperature reaches 21°C (70°F), add the yeast and stir.
5 Cover and store the mixture in a warm place for 4 days.
6 Transfer the mixture to a fermentation vessel with a fitted airlock.
7 After 2 months the mixture should be clear and ready to be bottled.

### NETTLE NEWS
• In Ancient Rome and Greece, doctors would use nettles to treat paralysed or rheumatic joints.
• Nettle tea is also good for treating liver problems.

### PRICKLY CUSTOMER
• Wear a pair of thick gloves when picking the nettles – unless you suffer from arthritis that is, for an old folklore states the sting is beneficial.
• Use a dock leaf to relieve an unwanted nettle sting.

# OAK LEAF WINE

### Ingredients
4.5 litres oak leaves
4.5 litres water
1 kg sugar
juice and grated zest of
    3 oranges
2.5 g wine yeast
1 tsp pectin enzyme
**Mature for:** 1 week
**Drink within:** 1 month

### Method
**1** Put the oak leaves in a bucket and pour in 4.5 litres boiling water. Leave overnight.
**2** Strain out the leaves.
**3** Boil the liquid for 20 minutes.
**4** Add the sugar, orange juice and grated zest to the liquid.

**5** Once the liquid has cooled down, add the yeast and leave uncovered for 5 days.
**6** Transfer to a fermentation jar with fitted airlock and leave to ferment.
**7** When the sediment settles, syphon off into a jar and add pectin enzyme.
**8** Leave for 24 hours and then filter into bottles. Seal with corks that have been boiled for 10 minutes. This wine is best consumed while it is young.

### ROYAL OAK
• Oak tree branches feature on the Estonian coat of arms.
• There are over 600 species of oak tree.

# PART 3

# SUMMER

# BREWING IN SUMMER

Once summer arrives the temptation to while away the day with a glass of something fruity and refreshing or golden and sparkling is strong. Beer, lager, cider, wine and mead are all excellent rewards at the end of a long day at work, and even more enjoyable if home-brewed.

## BEER AND LAGER

Light bitter and lagers are perfect refreshments on a hot summer's day. While no beers are brewed specifically for summer, certain types are particularly suited to the weather and the generally lighter food of the season. English mild (page 59) is a low-gravity beer that is light in both taste and alcohol content. It has been enjoyed since the 17th century, but its popularity increased in the 1950s when beer-drinkers started to favour bitters and lagers.

Ginger ale (page 60) originated in Britain and has been brewed since the 18th century. Fresh root ginger is used in this recipe and can be bought or home-grown. The fiery mix of savoury and sweet flavours makes this drink a real summertime refresher.

Raspberry beer (page 61), or framboise, is a Belgian beer made from fermented raspberries. Look out for bright red raspberries as these are just ripe. Dark raspberries will be very sweet.

Summertime India Pale Ale (page 62) is a variation on the pale ale style. India pale ales were first brewed in the UK in the 18th century. They are medium strength and taste hoppy and malty.

Weizen (page 63) and Belgian Wit Beer (page 58), are wheat beers reminiscent of Berlin-style beers. The finished beer has a thick head and a hazy body – a perfect drink to cool down with on a hot day.

Just saying 'golden lager' conjures up a mouth-watering image of sparkling amber liquid in a pint glass. The recipe on page 64 produces a cool lager which does exactly what drinks in this season should do: quench your thirst.

## CIDER

Cider suits the summer season as its fruity taste and cheekily high alcohol content complement lazy afternoons in the sun. However, this is the season when you will almost certainly have run out of apples from winter, so while you wait for autumn's supply of fruit to appear, try brewing turbo cider (page 65). All you need is apple juice and yeast. If you didn't manage to freeze some pressed apple juice from the previous season you can cheat and buy some from a supermarket.

## MEAD AND COUNTRY WINE

Midsummer mead (page 66) is called just that because it encapsulates the tastes and smells of summer. During preparation you will notice the strong scent coming from the meadowsweet (*Filipendula ulmaria*) leaves and woodruff (*Galium odoratum*) sprigs. In Britain during the Middle Ages and through to the 18th century, meadowsweet leaves were used as a 'strewing herb', a primitive version of an air freshener. From poor houses to royal castles, floors were covered in fragrant leaves and herbs to mask the smells of a country that hadn't yet mastered hygiene. Woodruff is also strongly scented, and so the end result is a refreshing drink with a summery aroma. Meadowsweet mostly grows in meadows and is in bloom between June and early September. Woodruff can be found in shady areas such as woodland.

Blackcurrants (page 67) start appearing in June and July. Pick them on a dry day, since they will deteriorate quickly and are at a greater risk of going mouldy if they are wet. They hold the most flavour a week after they have turned blue-black.

Cherries (page 68) come into season in at the end of June and are available for roughly six weeks. Pick cherries that are plump, glossy, and firm to the touch. Don't pick any that are wrinkled or mushy, as these are signs they will become mouldy.

The courgette is a vegetable that you'd never think could be drunk. On the contrary, it is a vegetable that can get you very drunk! The recipe for courgotto wino in this section (page 69) produces a drink with an alcohol content of 10%.

Another berry wine that tastes of summertime is gooseberry wine (page 70). Gooseberries are in season during June and July, so this is the time to pick the juiciest ones you can find. Wear gloves and long sleeves when harvesting gooseberries as the stems are covered in sharp thorns. Gooseberries make a lovely wine, best paired with a classic dessert such as gooseberry fool.

Honeysuckle (*Lonicera*) blooms in June and is best gathered when the flowers are open and when the weather is dry and sunny. Pick only the flowers – avoid the stems and berries. See page 71 for a honeysuckle wine recipe.

Lavender (*Lavandula*) flowers have a unique aroma and are a striking purple colour. Lavender is used for all sorts of things; to help you sleep, as cake decorations, to subtly scent a room, as a natural wedding confetti, as an antiseptic – it was even used to scent Roman baths. There is something so aesthetically pleasing about this flower you could eat it. So why not drink it? Lavender wine has quite a strong aroma so it may not be to everyone's taste, but this fresh and fragrant beverage is certainly worth a try; see page 72 for the recipe. Gather extra lavender and store for December's lavender-infused vodka (page 137).

Pea pods are very tasty in this season and while they may seem like an odd ingredient to brew with, the recipe on page 73 produces a medium, German-style wine.

Plum wine (page 74) is another delicious summer wine. A common complaint, however, is that the finished beverage can lack body. To combat this, throw a banana into the fermentation bucket along with the plums. This will increase the body without affecting the taste.

A fruit strongly associated with summer and the healthy feeling the sunshine brings is the strawberry (page 75). This is one of the most appealing fruits, with its bright red colour and unique taste and smell. Collect extra strawberries while they are in season and store them for the bellini cocktails recommended on page 137. To store strawberries and keep them in optimum condition, ensure that those you intend to freeze are bright red with vibrantly green stalks. Avoid any that show signs of decay as they won't improve from freezing. Gently wash them and then arrange on a baking tray, making sure they are not touching each other. Place the tray in the fridge and leave for an hour, and then place in the freezer overnight. Then transfer to an airtight container and return to the freezer.

# BELGIAN WIT BEER

## Ingredients

water

225 g cracked unmalted
    wheat

225 g flaked oats

1.5 kg light liquid malt
    extract

1 kg dry wheat malt extract

28 g Saaz hops

20 g Goldings hops

1 tsp crushed coriander
    seeds

zest of 2 oranges

11 g Belgian wit yeast

190 g cane sugar, for bottle
    conditioning

**Mature for:** 1 month

**Drink within:** 6 months

## Method

**1** Heat 2 litres of water to
65°C (149°F).

**2** Place the wheat and oats
inside a sparge bag and
steep in the water for 30
minutes.

**3** Rinse the sparge bag with
1 litre of water and discard.

**4** Add the extracts, 14 g
Saaz hops and 20 g Goldings
hops to 8 litres of water and
boil for 60 minutes.

**5** Forty-five minutes in to the
boil, add the remaining 14 g
of Saaz hops, the coriander
seeds and orange zest.

**6** Allow the mixture to cool
down and then strain into a
fermontor, topping up the
volume with water to reach
23 litres.

**7** Pitch the yeast and
ferment at 21°C (70°F) for
14 days.

**8** Bulk prime with 190 g of
cane sugar prior to bottling.

# ENGLISH MILD
༚༚

## Ingredients

3 kg pale malt

230 g crystal malt 50–60 L

170 g crystal malt 135–165 L

60 g chocolate malt

14 litres water

20 g Willamette hops

15 g Fuggles hops

11 g English ale yeast

50 g cane sugar, for bottle
conditioning

**Mature for:** 1 month

**Drink within:** 6 months

## Method

**1** Mash all grains in 14 litres of water at 67°C (152°F).

**2** After 60 minutes, reduce the temperature to 65°C (149°F) and do starch tests (see panel).

**3** Sparge with 12 litres of water heated to 75°C (167°F).

**4** Add the Willamette hops and boil for 60 minutes.

**5** Thirty minutes in to the boil, add the Fuggles hops.

**6** When the 60 minutes is up, allow the wort to cool.

**7** Transfer to a fermenter and when the temperature drops to 21°C (70°F), pitch the yeast.

**8** Leave to ferment for 2 weeks.

**9** Bulk prime with 50 g of cane sugar prior to bottling.

### STARCH TEST

When mashing at 65°C (149°F) all starch in the wort should have converted into sugar after an hour, but you need to do a starch test to confirm this. Take a liquid sample, making sure you don't collect any solids with it, and put it on a white plate. Add 2 drops of tincture of iodine to the sample; if it turns blue-black, the starches have not been fully converted. Keep mashing and test a further sample. If the next sample does not change colour, the wort is fully converted.

# GINGER ALE

୧୦୧

Since the fermentation process is stopped after a few days by refrigerating this ginger ale, the alcohol content in it will be extremely low.

## Ingredients

40 g fresh root ginger, finely grated

170 g white sugar

2 litres water

¼ tsp brewer's yeast

2 tbsp lemon juice

**Mature for:** 2 weeks

**Drink within:** 3 months

## Method

**1** Combine the ginger, sugar and 125 ml of the water in a saucepan and heat gently, stirring until the sugar has dissolved.

**2** Remove from the heat. Cover and leave to steep for 1 hour.

**3** Pour the syrup through a strainer, making sure no juice is left in the mixture. Place the syrup in the fridge to chill.

**4** Once it has chilled, pour the syrup into a 2 litre plastic bottle using a funnel.

**4** Add the yeast, lemon juice and remaining water to the bottle.

**6** Secure the bottle with its lid and shake gently. Store the bottle at 19–23°C (66–73°F) for 48 hours and then transfer to the fridge for 2 weeks.

---

### STOMACH-SOOTHER

All over the world, ginger is used to help relieve the symptoms of nausea.

---

60

# RASPBERRY BEER

## Ingredients

1.5 kg crystal malt 40 L
water
1.35 kg light dry malt extract
225 g dextrine malt
28 g Goldings hops
340 g cane sugar
1 kg raspberries, washed
11 g Belgian ale yeast
170 g cane sugar, for bottle
    conditioning

**Mature for:** 2 months
**Drink within:** 6 months

## Method

**1** Steep the crystal malt in
8 litres of water at 65°C (150°F)
for 45 minutes.
**2** Add the light dry malt
extract, dextrine malt and
14 g Goldings hops and boil
for 40 minutes.
**3** Add the sugar, raspberries
and remaining hops. Boil for
10 minutes.
**4** Allow the mixture to chill
and then strain into a
fermenting bin. Top up the
volume with water to 15 litres.
**5** Pitch the yeast and ferment
for 7 days at 21°C (70°F).
**6** Monitor the fermentation
process and when it slows,
rack to a secondary fermenter.
**7** Leave for a week and then
bulk prime with 170 g of cane
sugar and bottle.

### RASPBERRY SPECIAL

In the late 1950s raspberries
were taken from Scotland to
London on a train known as
the Raspberry Special.

# SUMMERTIME INDIA PALE ALE

## Ingredients

4 kg pale malt

water

300 g crystal malt

200 g dextrine malt

56 g oak chips

2 tsp gypsum

35 g Goldings hops

1 tsp Irish moss

11 g American ale yeast

**Mature for:** 2 months

**Drink within:** 6 months

## Method

**1** Mash the pale malt in 13 litres of water at 67°C (153°F) for 30–60 minutes. Start starch tests after 30 minutes (see p.59).

**2** Add the crystal and dextrine malts to the mash and increase the temperature to 75°C (167°F). Mash out for 10 minutes and then sparge with 10 litres of water at 75°C (167°F). Bring to the boil.

**3** Add the oak chips to a saucepan and cover with water. Boil for 10 minutes.

**4** Strain the liquid into your wort and add the gypsum.

**5** After 30 minutes, add 14 g Goldings hops.

**6** After 45 minutes add a further 14 g Goldings hops along with the Irish moss. Boil for 15 minutes.

**7** Allow the mixture to cool down and then pitch the yeast.

**0** Dry hop (see below) in the secondary fermenter with 7 g Goldings hops. Leave to ferment for 7 days, then rack off and leave to ferment for a further week before bottling.

### DRY HOPPING

Dry hopping is the process of adding hops to the wort after boiling. This adds aroma and flavour without adding any bitterness.

# WEIZEN

This Bavarian beverage has been brewed since the 16th century.

## Ingredients
water
1.35 kg wheat malt
1 tbsp gypsum
1.5 kg liquid amber malt
  extract
1.35 kg light dry malt extract
42 g Hallertauer hops
9 g Willamette hops
11 g ale yeast
140 g cane sugar, for bottle
  conditioning
**Mature for:** 2 months
**Drink within:** 6 months

## Method
**1** Heat 3 litres of water to 75°C (167°F). Add the grains and gypsum.
**2** Bring the temperature down to 65°C (149°F).
**3** Mash the liquid for 1 hour.
**4** Strain out the grains, pouring the water into a second pot.
**5** Heat 2 litres of water to 75°C (167°F) and rinse the grains with it.
**6** Add the malt extracts and Hallertauer hops to the water and boil for 30 minutes.
**7** Twenty-eight minutes in to the boil add the Willamette hops.
**8** Put 8 litres of water into your fermenter and add the hot wort. Top up the water so the volume reaches 23 litres.
**9** When the wort temperature is 25–27°C (77–81°F), pitch the yeast. Cover the mixture and attach the airlock.
**10** Leave to ferment for 10 days, then rack and leave to ferment for a further 4 days.
**11** Bulk prime with 140 g of cane sugar before bottling.

# GOLDEN LAGER

## Ingredients

water

2.75 kg light malt extract

28 g Willamette hops

14 g Perle hops

1 tsp Irish moss

14 g Cascade hops

11 g lager yeast

100 g cane sugar, for bottle
conditioning

**Mature for:** 3 months

**Drink within:** 6 months

## Method

**1** Heat 8 litres of water in a pot until just boiling.

**2** Remove the pot from the heat and add the light malt extract, Willamette and Perle hops (in a hop bag). Return to the heat and boil for 60 minutes.

**3** Forty-five minutes in to the boil, add the Irish moss.

**4** Fifty-eight minutes in to the boil, add the Cascade hops to the hop bag and boil for the remaining 2 minutes.

**5** Fill the fermenting bin with 12 litres of cold water.

**6** Strain the wort into the fermenter. Top up the volume with cold water to make 19 litres and pitch the yeast.

**7** Leave to ferment for 15 minutes and then transfer to a fermenting vessel and fit with an airlock.

**8** Store the lager in a dark place for 1 week.

**9** When bubbles stop forming on the top of the lager, fermentation has stopped.

**10** Bulk prime with 100 g of cane sugar and bottle.

### LAGER LOVERS

Since the 1950s, lager has become more popular than traditional ale.

# TURBO CIDER

## Ingredients

4.5 litres pure apple juice

5 g yeast

1 Campden tablet, crushed

**Mature for:** 6 months

**Drink within:** 1 year

## Method

**1** Pour 3 litres of apple juice along with the yeast into a demijohn.

**2** Seal with a bung and airlock. Shake the demijohn and leave to ferment for 36 hours.

**3** Add the rest of the apple juice.

**4** Leave to ferment. Monitor the final gravity as it needs to be constant for three days – the reading should be 9.98. Add one crushed Campden tablet to maintain this reading.

> **TURBO TIP**
> Adding 80 g sugar or 2–3 teaspoons of honey at step 1 will create a stronger cider.

# MIDSUMMER MEAD

## Ingredients

5 litres water

500 ml meadowsweet leaves

500 ml woodruff sprigs

500 ml heather flowers

3 cloves

500 ml honey

90 g brown sugar

500 g barley malt

2.5 g wine yeast

**Mature for:** 1 year

**Drink within:** 1 year

## Method

**1** Bring the water to the boil and add the meadowsweet, woodruff, heather and cloves. Allow to boil for 1 hour and then add the honey, brown sugar and barley malt. Stir so that the sugar and honey dissolve.

**2** Cover with aluminium foil and leave to cool to 37°C (99°F).

**3** Transfer the mixture to a demijohn and add the yeast.

**4** Seal the demijohn with a bung and fit an airlock. Store in a warm area.

**5** The airlock should start bubbling and foam will form on the top of the liquid. Store for 2 weeks and monitor the bubbles, which should begin to slow down.

**6** When the sediment is between 2–3 cm, rack off to a secondary fermenting vessel.

**7** Top up with fresh water and refit the bung and airlock, exposing the mead to as little oxygen as possible.

**8** Check the mead daily and repeat the racking process as the sediment builds up again. Top up as necessary.

**9** When the bubbling has ceased entirely the fermentation is complete.

**10** Bottle and leave to mature for one year.

# BLACKCURRANT WINE

## Ingredients

1.3 kg blackcurrants

1.3 kg white sugar

4.5 litres water

1 tsp citric acid

2.5 g wine yeast

4 tsp yeast nutrient

**Mature for:** 1 year

**Drink within:** 1 year

## Method

**1** Crush the blackcurrants and place in a fermentation bucket.

**2** Boil the sugar in the water. Pour over the blackcurrants.

**3** Allow the mixture to cool and then add the citric acid, wine yeast and yeast nutrient and cover.

**4** Store the mixture for 5 days, stirring daily.

**5** Strain the liquid through a muslin into a demijohn with a fitted airlock.

**6** Store in a warm area to ferment for 2 months.

**7** When fermentation has finished, rack the wine into a clean container and store in a cool area for 2 months.

**8** Syphon into bottles when the wine is clear.

---

### TOP TIP

Leave this wine to mature for a year before drinking.

# CHERRY WINE

ᘔᘔ

## Ingredients

1.5 kg cherries, stalks removed

5 litres unchlorinated water

1.5 kg granulated sugar

juice and grated zest of
  2 lemons

2 tsp yeast nutrient

2.5 g wine yeast

**Mature for:** 6–12 months

**Drink within:** 1 year

## Method

**1** Place the cherries in a fermenting bucket and cover with 3.5 litres of boiling water.

**2** Mash roughly and allow the temperature to cool.

**3** Mash the fruit again and then cover. Store for 3 days.

**4** Strain the fruit through a muslin, extracting as much juice as possible into the fermentation bucket.

**5** In a separate bucket, boil the remaining water and add the sugar.

**6** When the mixture has cooled, add the lemon juice, grated lemon zest and yeast nutrient.

**7** Check the temperature and when it is at 30°C (86°F) add the yeast and stir.

**8** Combine the yeast mixture with the cherry mixture and cover. Store in a warm area for 3 days.

**9** Pour into a demijohn and top up with water. Seal with a bung and airlock and store for 3 months.

**10** Rack off into a secondary container and seal. Store for a further month.

**11** Rack into bottles and store in a cool area for 6 months to a year before drinking.

### CHERRY PICKING

In William Shakespeare's *A Midsummer Night's Dream*, cherries symbolize love and romance.

# COURGETTE WINE

## Ingredients

6–8 courgettes

28 g root ginger

170 g raisins, chopped

4.5 litres water

juice of 2 lemons

juice of 1 orange

2.5 g wine yeast

1 tsp yeast nutrient

900 g white sugar

**Mature for:** 6 months

**Drink within:** 1 year

## Method

**1** Combine the courgettes with the ginger and raisins. Mash together.

**2** Cover with 4.5 litres of boiling water and stir.

**3** When the mixture has cooled, add the juice from the lemons and orange, the yeast and yeast nutrient.

**4** Leave to ferment for 4 days in a fermentation bin with fitted airlock.

**5** Strain the mixture and stir in the sugar. Refit the airlock.

**6** Leave to ferment until the bubbles stop appearing and then bottle the wine.

---

### COURGETTE COUNTDOWN

Courgettes will only keep for 5 days in the fridge, so use them quickly. Keep them in a paper bag rather than in plastic.

### THE CURCURBITA FAMILY

Courgettes are part of the same family as marrows, pumpkins, cucumbers and watermelons.

# GOOSEBERRY WINE

## Ingredients

2.2 kg gooseberries, stalks
   removed
4.5 litres water
½ tsp pectin enzyme
1.3 kg white sugar
1 Campden tablet, crushed
2.5 g wine yeast
1 tsp yeast nutrient
½ tsp potassium sorbate
**Mature for:** 6 months
**Drink within:** 1 year

## Method

**1** Put the gooseberries in a
large pan and mash,
breaking the skins.
**2** Boil the water and pour it
over the pulp.
**3** Add the pectin enzyme,
sugar and Campden tablet to
the pulp and stir, dissolving
the sugar. Cover and leave for
24 hours.
**4** Add the yeast and yeast
nutrient and stir. Cover again
and leave for 5–6 days.

**5** Strain the mixture.
**6** Pour into a demijohn and fit
with an airlock. Leave to
ferment for 3–4 weeks.
**7** Syphon off the wine and
discard the sediment.
**8** Leave for 2 months and then
syphon again. Repeat this
step twice more.
**9** Add the potassium sorbate
and then decant into bottles.

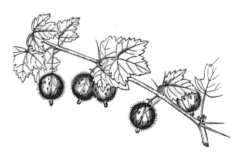

### GOOSEBERRY GOSSIP

Leave this wine to mature for
6 months before drinking as
the depth of flavour will
continue to improve.

# HONEYSUCKLE FLOWER WINE

## Ingredients

1.1 litres honeysuckle flowers
1.3 kg white sugar
2 oranges
225 g raisins
2 tsp acid blend
1 tsp pectin enzyme
1 Campden tablet, crushed
1 tsp tannin
1 tsp yeast nutrient
4.5 litres cooled boiled water
2.5 g wine yeast
**Mature for:** 6 months
**Drink within:** 1 year

## Method

**1** Rinse the flowers in cold water, then place them in a fermentation bucket.

**2** Combine all the ingredients except the wine yeast with the water.

**3** Stir the mixture and when the sugar has dissolved, leave to stand for 12 hours.

**4** Add the wine yeast.

**5** For the next 4 days, stir the mixture in the morning and evening.

**6** Strain the mixture and transfer to a demijohn with an airlock.

**7** After 6 weeks, syphon off the wine.

**8** Within the next year, syphon off 2–3 more times, until the wine is clear. Decant into bottles.

### HONEYTRAP

Honeysuckle is sometimes placed inside cat toys because cats are attracted to the scent.

### HONEYSUCKLE HINTS

• Once you've bottled this wine, leave it for 6 months for optimum taste.
• Use the flowers only as the berries are poisonous.

# LAVENDER WINE

## Ingredients
4.5 litres water
125 ml dried lavender flowers, off stem
juice of 1 lemon
1.1 kg sugar
1 litre white grape concentrate
1 tsp yeast nutrient
2.5 g wine yeast
**Mature for:** 2 months
**Drink within:** 6 months

## Method
**1** Pour 1.1 litres of boiling water over the lavender flowers. Add the lemon juice, cover and leave for 3 days.
**2** Strain the mixture into a demijohn.
**3** Dissolve the sugar in hot water and add to the jar, along with the grape concentrate, yeast nutrient and yeast.
**4** Fit an airlock and leave to ferment for 2 weeks, or longer if the wine has not cleared.

**5** Once fermentation has finished and the wine is clear, rack and store for a further 3 months before bottling.

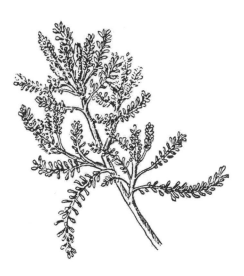

### LAVENDER LESSONS
• Lavender is part of the mint family.
• It is an ecologically good plant to have in your garden as it attracts bees.

# PEA POD WINE
ภวน

## Ingredients

900 g empty pea pods
4.5 litres water
450 g sultanas, chopped
1 kg sugar
284 ml freshly made strong tea
15 ml citric acid
juice of 2 oranges
2.5 g wine yeast
1 tsp yeast nutrient
few drops of pectin enzyme
**Mature for**: 6 months
**Drink within**: 1 year

## Method

**1** Cut the pea pods into small pieces. Put them in sufficient water to cover them, bring to the boil slowly and simmer for 20 minutes with the lid on.
**2** Put the sultanas in a fermenting bucket with the sugar. Strain the boiling pea pods over the sugar and sultanas. Squeeze out as much liquid as you can, then discard the pods.
**3** Stir the mixture and add 4.5 litres of boiling water. Ensure the sugar has dissolved. Add the tea and citric acid and cover. The temperature needs to cool to 18°C (64°F) now.
**4** Stir the orange juice into the mixture. Add the yeast and yeast nutrient along with a few drops of pectin enzyme.
**5** Cover the fermenting bucket with a lid. Store for 10 days in a warm place, stirring daily.
**6** Strain out all the solids.
**7** Rinse out the fermenting bucket and return the strained liquid to it. Cover and store as before and leave to ferment for 3–4 days.
**8** Transfer into a 4.5 litre jar, trying to keep back as much residue as you can. Fill the jar to the neck with cooled, pre-boiled water.
**9** Fit an airlock and leave until fermentation has stopped before bottling.

# PLUM WINE

Plum wine is rich and smooth, with a taste and aroma that are often appreciated by people who don't normally care for alcoholic drinks.

## Ingredients
4.5 litres water
2.2 kg plums, chopped
1.3 kg white sugar
1 tsp citric acid
2.5 g wine yeast
**Mature for.** 6–8 months
**Drink within:** 1 year

## Method
**1** Boil the water and pour it into a fermentation bucket. Add the chopped plums to the bucket. Cover and store for 4 days, stirring twice a day.
**2** Put the sugar in a secondary bucket and strain the plum liquid over it. Discard the plums. Stir the mixture until the sugar has dissolved. Add the citric acid.
**3** Add the yeast and cover.
**4** Over the next 5 days, stir intermittently.
**5** Pour into a fermentation bottle with a fitted airlock.
**6** When fermentation has finished, syphon the wine into bottles and store in a cool area for 6–8 months to mature.

### ORIENTAL WINES
Plum wine is popular in Japan, Korea and China. The Taiwanese version *wumeijiu* is mixed with oolong tea.

### FRUIT FACT
Plums are good for you – they are a great source of Vitamins A and C and have antioxidant properties.

# STRAWBERRY WINE

## Ingredients

1.5 kg fresh strawberries,
   hulled
4.5 litres boiling water
juice of ½ lemon
1.1 kg white sugar
2.5 g yeast
1 tsp yeast nutrient
**Mature for:** 1 year
**Drink within:** 1 year

## Method

**1** Mash the strawberries in a bucket and then cover with the boiling water and lemon juice. Stir vigorously for 2 minutes.

**2** Cover with a linen cloth and store in a cool, dark area for 1 week. Stir daily.

**3** Strain the mixture into a bowl and discard the pulp.

**4** Add the sugar to the strawberries and stir.

**5** Once the sugar has dissolved, add the yeast and yeast nutrient. Pour into another bucket and leave for 1 week to stand. Stir daily.

**6** Transfer the liquid into demijohns and fit airlocks. Store in a cool, dark area for 3 months.

**7** When fermentation has finished and the wine is clear, pour into bottles and cork.

### GAME, SET, MATCH!

In Britain, roughly 27,000 kg of strawberries and 7,000 litres of cream are consumed during the Wimbledon Championships every year by tennis fans.

### MAD ABOUT STRAWBERRIES

In the 14th century, Charles V of France ordered that 1,200 strawberry plants be grown in the Royal Gardens of the Louvre.

# PART 4

# AUTUMN

# BREWING IN AUTUMN

༄ঌ

For many people, autumn means a return to reality as the summer holidays come to an end and the kids go back to school. The weather gets ever windier and colder and whether you like it or not, the shops are telling you it's the countdown to Christmas and the rush to make last-minute purchases in crowded shops. However, there is much to look forward to in this season, not least the glories of autumn foliage on crisp, bright mornings, scarlet rosehips in the hedgerows and nuts and berries on the trees. Halloween and Bonfire Night are both festive occasions, and what better way to celebrate them than by serving some drinks that reflect the smells and colours of the season?

## BEER

In autumn, the world-famous annual beer festival Oktoberfest takes place in Munich, Germany. First held in 1810 to celebrate the marriage of Crown Prince Ludwig of Bavaria, it lasts for 16 days and each year an estimated 6,900,000 litres of beer are consumed. The event is so popular it has been replicated in cities and towns worldwide. Dubbel (page 82) is a brown ale with red tones. It is rich and earthy, similar to the Dunkelweizen (page 83), both being dark beers which are typical of the Oktoberfest style of beers. Dunkel means 'dark' in German – which is reflected in dunkelweizen's dark chestnut brown colour and roasted wheat flavour.

In England, brewers tend to

create beers of medium strength which have deep red or nut brown colours during the autumn season. Nut brown ale (page 84) is a smooth, walnut-coloured beer that tastes of honey, malt and aromatic hops.

Oatmeal stout (page 85) is an autumnal warmer which has been brewed for centuries. The high oat content can lead to a strong, bitter flavour which is the reason its popularity waned during the 16th century. It made a comeback, however, some three hundred years later in the 19th century when positive associations were made between oat products such as porridge and good health. In the modern version, the oat flavours are not so apparent and instead the beer tastes toasty and sweet.

If you're having a Halloween party this autumn, be sure to brew a cauldron full of pumpkin ale (page 86). Pumpkins can be shop-bought or easily home-grown. Pick pumpkins that have cracked stems and tough skin, as these are signs they are ready to be eaten – or, in this case, mashed and turned into beer.

**CIDER AND PERRY**

Autumn is the time to harvest your apples and pears. If you want to enjoy them throughout the other seasons, now is also the time to store them. They need to be picked before the first frost, so plan ahead and harvest them before the weather turns seriously cold.

To check that apples and pears are ready for picking, place a cupped hand underneath each fruit and gently twist it away from the branch. Like most fruit, if it comes off with hardly any force, then it is ripe. To store, roughly wrap the apples and pears individually in newspaper. Keep them in a cool, frost-free environment such as a garage or garden shed. If you want to create ciders and perries during this season you'll need to get your bounty pulped and pressed soon after harvesting. Recipes for delicious ciders and perries are on pages 87–89.

## MEAD AND COUNTRY WINES

Blackberries are ready to be harvested in early autumn and can be made into delicious desserts and jams as well as mead and wine. Pick blackberries that are black and feel plump. When dropping them into your bucket, don't be tempted to overfill it or press them down to make more room; blackberries are quite tough but you don't want to risk prematurely squashing the ones at the bottom. Look between stems for hidden blackberries, as these are often missed. The juice will stain, so avoid the berries coming into contact with your clothing. There are three recipes using blackberries in

this section: mead (page 90), blackberry wine (page 92), and blackberry and elderflower wine (page 93).

Barley wine (page 91) is technically a beer, as it uses grains, not fruit, but it has this name regardless. Barley wines vary in colour from golden copper to dark brown and generally have a medium-high alcohol content.

Clover wine (page 94) uses red clovers (*Trifolium pratense*) which must be picked early in the morning, once the dew has dried up. Red clovers are used in a variety of natural medicine recipes, and are believed to relieve symptoms of bronchitis and asthma.

Hawthorn (*Crataegus oxyacantha*) berries begin to ripen in September and can be harvested as late as November. Hawthorn leaves and berries have been picked for use in cooking and brewing for centuries. The berries are known to have properties which are good for the heart, while a tea made from dried berries is said to calm an unsettled stomach. A healthy haw wine (page 95) can be made by boiling the berries in water, along with two oranges and a lemon.

Loganberries (*Rubus loganobaccus*) are a hybrid fruit, a cross between a blackberry and a raspberry. They start to appear in the beginning of autumn and the best ones to pick are dark red in colour. The flavour is stronger and sharper than that of raspberries. See page 96 for a tasty recipe.

While you're making perries this autumn, leave some pears aside to make a delicious pear wine (page 97). The flavour will depend on which type of pear you use as they differ in sweetness, so you may need to experiment before you find a variety to your taste.

You might be surprised to learn that the potato is another ingredient that works very well in wine-making – and this also solves what to do with any potatoes you've dug up that are too small to cook (see page 98). Make sure you cut out any eyes or green bits as these are toxic.

Rosehip wine (page 99) is made from the wild dog rose (*Rosa canina*). The hips are ready to be picked when they have ripened to red as summer turns to autumn. It is recommended that you leave rosehip wine to mature for one year after brewing.

Rowan trees (*Sorbus*) are common throughout the northern hemisphere and their berries have been used for wine for centuries. The berries are at their best in October; see page 100 for the recipe.

Sloes, the fruit of the blackthorn bush, are most often used to make sloe gin (page 139) but they work well in wine too (see page 101). Pick sloes after the first frost and watch out for the thorns.

# DUBBEL

ɷɷ

## Ingredients

water
115 g crystal malt 10 L
115 g brown malt
3 kg light liquid malt extract
28 g Goldings hops
½ tsp Irish moss
14 g Hallertauer hops
1 kg light dry malt extract
450 g Belgian candi sugar
Trappist ale yeast
70 g cane sugar, for bottle
conditioning
**Mature for:** 3 months
**Drink within:** 6 months

## Method

**1** Heat 8 litres of water to 65°C (149°F) and steep the grains for 30 minutes.
**2** Remove the grains using a strainer and bring the water to a boil. When the water starts to boil, take the wort off the heat and add 450 g light liquid malt extract. Stir.
**3** Return to the heat and allow the wort to boil again. Add the Goldings hops. Boil for 60 minutes.
**4** After the first 15 minutes, add the Irish moss.
**5** At 57 minutes, add the Hallertauer hops.
**6** Once the 60 minutes are up, add the remaining light liquid malt extract, light dry malt extract and Belgian candi sugar and stir. Leave for 10 minutes.
**7** Strain the wort into a fermenter and top up with 8 litres of cold water.
**8** Allow the temperature to cool to 25°C (77°F) and pitch the yeast.
**9** Leave to ferment for 5–7 days and then rack to a secondary fermenter for 2 weeks.
**10** Bulk prime with 70 g cane sugar for bottle conditioning.

# DUNKELWEIZEN

## Ingredients

2.75 kg wheat malt

1.8 kg Munich malt

450 g caraMunich malt 60 L water

14 g Hallertauer Herbrucker hops

14 g Tettnang hops

11 g Weizen yeast

180 g cane sugar, for bottle conditioning

**Mature for:** 2 months

**Drink within:** 6 months

## Method

**1** Put the crushed grains in the tun and pour in 8 litres of water at 75°C (167°F).

**2** Stabilize the temperature at 65°C (149°F) and mash for 90 minutes. Stir every 15 minutes.

**3** Sparge with 10 litres of water at 75°C (167°F).

**4** Sparge again with water at 75°C (167°F), using enough water to bring the volume up to 23 litres.

**5** Boil the wort for 30 minutes.

**6** Add the Hallertauer hops and boil for 30 minutes.

**7** Add the Tettnang hops and boil for a further 30 minutes.

**8** Allow the wort to cool to room temperature and rack off into a fermenter.

**9** Check the temperature of the wort. When it reaches 21°C (70°F), pitch the yeast.

**10** Ferment at 19°C (66°F) for 10 days.

**11** Rack and leave to ferment at 19°C (66°F) for 7 days.

**12** Bulk prime with 180 g of cane sugar before bottling.

**13** Condition the bottles for 1 week at room temperature and then for a further 5 days at 5°C (41°F).

# NUT BROWN ALE

## Ingredients

1.36 kg American 2-row malt
450 g Munich malt
500 g honey malt
450 g crystal malt 50-60 L
170 g chocolate malt
water
2.75 kg light dried malt extract
85 g Fuggles hops
11 g English ale yeast
70 g cane sugar for bottle
   conditioning
**Mature for:** 1 month
**Drink within:** 6 months

## Method

**1** Mash all the grains in 14 litres of water at a temperature of 67°C (153°F).
**2** After 50 minutes, start starch tests – see page 59 for more information.
**3** Batch sparge with 12 litres of water at 75°C (167°F).
**4** Transfer the wort to a fermenting vessel and add the malt extract and 45 g Fuggles hops. Top up the volume to 26 litres. Boil for 60 minutes.
**5** Forty minutes in to the boil, add the remaining 40 g of Fuggles hops.
**6** Allow the temperature to cool to 21°C (70°F) and pitch the yeast. Leave to ferment for 2 weeks.
**7** Bulk prime with 70 g of cane sugar and bottle.

### MINE'S A PINT

The term 'brown ale' was first employed to describe this style of beer in late 17th-century London.

# OATMEAL STOUT

## Ingredients

1 kg flaked oats
500 g crystal malt 120 L
500 g black patent malt
water
1.5 kg amber dry malt extract
1.5 kg dark dry malt extract
60 g Northdown hops
20 g Fuggles hops
11 g English ale yeast
70 g cane sugar, for bottle
   conditioning
**Mature for:** 3 months
**Drink within:** 6 months

## Method

**1** Steep the grains in a sparge bag in 5 litres of cold water. Bring to the boil. Simmer for 15 minutes and pour into the fermenting bin.
**2** Wash the grains through with cold water.
**3** Top up the volume to 8 litres and add the malt extracts and Northdown hops and boil. Forty-five minutes in to the boil, add the Fuggles hops.
**4** Allow to boil for 15 minutes and then cool. Sparge with enough water to increase the volume to 20 litres.
**5** Pitch the yeast and leave to ferment for 5–7 days.
**6** Rack to a secondary fermenter.
**7** Bulk prime with 70 g of cane sugar and bottle.

### DOCTOR'S ORDERS

In the past, oatmeal stout was recommended as a restorative drink for pregnant women, invalids and the elderly.

# PUMPKIN ALE
ରେ

## Ingredients

2.25 kg pumpkin

1 tsp gypsum

700 g pale malt

500 g crystal malt

water

3 kg liquid amber malt extract

50 g Willamette hops

1 tsp Irish moss

2 tsp ground cinnamon

1 tsp nutmeg

30 g chopped root ginger

11 g ale yeast

90 g cane sugar, for bottle
  conditioning

**Mature for:** 2 months

**Drink within:** 6 months

## Method

**1** Bake the pumpkin in the oven for 1 hour and 15 minutes at 180°C (350°F/Gas mark 4), or until the skin has caramelized.

**2** Remove the skin and crush the flesh.

**3** Put the pumpkin flesh, gypsum and grains into a fermenting bin and pour in 6 litres of water. Mash at 65°C (149°F) for 60 minutes.

**4** Strain into a bucket and sparge with 4 litres of water at 75°C (167°F). Return the wort to the fermenting bin.

**5** Add the malt extract and 30 g hops. Boil for 60 minutes.

**6** After 30 minutes in to the boil, add the Irish moss.

**7** Fifty minutes in to the boil, add the remaining hops.

**8** Fifty-five minutes in to the boil, add the spices and ginger.

**9** Take off the heat and leave to stand for a few minutes.

**10** Strain the wort into a fermenting bin and top up to 19 litres.

**11** When the temperature is 25–27°C (77–81°F), pitch the yeast.

**12** Rack off to a secondary bin.

**13** Bulk prime with 90 g cane sugar and bottle.

# SPARKLING DRY CIDER

## Ingredients

4.5 kg apples – sharp variety

2 kg apples – bitter sweet
   variety

2 kg apples – sweet variety

2.5 g champagne yeast

1 tsp sugar

1 Campden tablet, crushed

**Mature for:** 6 months

**Drink within:** 1 year

## Method

**1** Pulp the apples by pressing them yourself or taking them to be professionally pressed.

**2** Take 85 ml apple juice and add the yeast and sugar. Store in a warm area for 2 days.

**3** Add the Campden tablet to the remaining apple juice (about 4.5 litres) and put to one side for 2 days.

**4** After the 2 days are up, combine the two mixtures and allow fermentation to start.

**5** Using the hydrometer, check the gravity hourly until it reaches approximately 1005.

**6** Once the gravity is at 1005, bottle the cider. Add ½ tsp of sugar to each bottle and shake to dissolve.

### HOW D'YA LIKE THEM APPLES?

In the United Kingdom, some 600 million litres of cider is produced annually.

# SWEET CIDER

### Ingredients
4.5 kg apples
2.5 g champagne yeast
1 tsp sugar
2 Campden tablets, crushed
**Mature for:** 6 months
**Drink within:** 1 year

### Method
**1** Pulp the apples by pressing them yourself or taking them to be professionally pressed.
**2** Take 85 ml apple juice and add the yeast and sugar. Store in a warm area for 2 days.

**3** Add a Campden tablet to the remaining apple juice and put to one side for 2 days.
**4** After the 2 days are up, combine the mixtures and allow fermentation to start.
**5** Using the hydrometer, check the gravity; it should be about 1060.
**6** Store in a warm area until the gravity drops to 1020.
**7** Add the remaining Campden tablet to the cider and store for a further 2 weeks before bottling.

### HOLY CIDER
In the 14th century, children were often baptized in cider because it was cleaner than water.

# COUNTRY-STYLE PERRY

## Ingredients
10–12 large pears
**Mature for:** Serve immediately
**Drink within:** 1 year

## Method
**1** Place the pears in a warm area so they begin to soften.
**2** Chop and smash the fruit into a pulp.
**3** Strain through a muslin.
**4** Store the extracted juice in a warm place and allow to bubble.
**5** Monitor the juice and when the sediment drops to the bottom, transfer into a cask and cover. Leave to mature for 6–8 months.
**6** Strain and bottle.

### PERRY POINTER
Brewer's yeast can be added to the extracted juice if you don't want to rely on the natural yeast to do the job.

### POWERFUL PEARS
In Ancient Greece, pears were used to treat nausea.

# BLACKBERRY MEAD

ⳤⳤ

## Ingredients
1 kg fresh blackberries
5.7 kg honey
5 litres unchlorinated water
pared zest of 2 oranges
4 tsp yeast nutrient
6 tsp pectin enzyme
2.5 g wine yeast
**Mature for:** 6-8 months
**Drink within:** 1 year

## Method
**1** Boil the blackberries in 3 kg honey and 2 litres of water until soft.
**2** Put the remaining unchlorinated water and honey in a separate pan.
**3** Stir until the honey dissolves and then add the blackberry mixture.
**4** Add the orange zest and yeast nutrient and pour the mixture into a fermenting bucket.
**5** Cover the fermenting bucket and leave to cool to room temperature.
**6** Add the pectin enzyme and store for 12 hours.
**7** Add the yeast, cover again and store in a warm, dark area for 8 days.
**8** Stir daily until vigorous fermentation calms.
**9** Strain the mixture into a demijohn and top up the volume to 5 litres with water.
**10** Fit a bung and fermentation lock and return to the warm, dark area to ferment for 60–90 days, or until fermentation has stopped.
**11** Rack the wine into a secondary fermenting container, add a bung and lock and store for 45 days.
**12** Rack again and store for a further 45 days.
**13** Rack the mead into bottles and secure with corks.

# BARLEY WINE

## Ingredients
water
900 g diastatic malt extract
250 g pale malt
250 g crystal malt
juice of 1 lemon
100 g brown sugar
25 g Goldings hops
2.5 g champagne yeast
15 g cane sugar, for bottle
   conditioning
**Mature for**: 1 year
**Drink within**: 1 year

## Method
**1** Heat 2 litres of water to 75°C (167°F) and add the extract and malts. Pour the liquid into a mash tun for 60 minutes.
**2** Strain out the wort and sparge the grains with 2 litres of water at 75°C (167°F).
**3** Stir in the lemon, sugar and hops and boil for 60 minutes.
**4** Remove from the heat and allow to rest for 15 minutes.
Transfer the wort to a fermenting bin.
**5** Strain the liquid and solids through a sparge bag, rinsing through with 500 ml of water at 75°C (167°F). Squeeze the solids to get all the diluted sugars out.
**6** Top up the fermenter to 4.5 litres. When the temperature is 36–40°C (97–104°F), pitch the yeast, leave for 20 minutes and store in a warm area to begin fermentation.
**7** When activity subsides, rack off to a demijohn and store for 12 days.
**8** Bulk prime with 15 g cane sugar and store the bottles for 2 weeks at 20–25°C (68–77°F), then leave to mature for 50 weeks in a cool area.

# BLACKBERRY WINE

## Ingredients

2 kg blackberries, stems and
    leaves removed
water
1 Campden tablet, crushed
1 kg white sugar
2.5 g red wine yeast
**Mature for:** 1 year
**Drink within:** 1 year

## Method

**1** Crush the blackberries in a
plastic bucket. Add 1.2 litres
pre-boiled, cooled water to
cover them and mix.
**2** Crush a Campden tablet
and dissolve in warm water,
then add to the berry mix.
Leave for 2 hours.
**3** Boil 330 g sugar in 1.7 litres
of water for 1 minute, then
allow to cool to room
temperature, forming a
sugar syrup.
**4** In a separate container, add
the yeast to 113 ml of warm
water and leave for 10 minutes.
**5** Combine the sugar syrup
with the berry mix. Add the
yeast and cover. Leave in a
warm place for 7 days.
**6** Strain the liquid and discard
the pulp.
**7** Strain the wine into a 4.5
litre demijohn.
**8** Boil 330 g sugar in 500 ml of
water and leave to cool. Add
to the mixture once it cools to
room temperature.
**9** Seal the demijohn with an
airlock and store for 10 days.
**10** Syphon your wine into
another demijohn.
**11** Boil the remaining sugar in
the remaining water and
allow to cool. Add to the
demijohn and seal with an
airlock. Store in a warm place.
**12** Once fermentation has
ceased syphon into another
demijohn, leaving the
sediment behind, and bottle.

# BLACKBERRY AND ELDERBERRY WINE

ख़ऌॄ

## Ingredients

1 kg elderberries, stems and
  leaves removed
1 kg blackberries, stems and
  leaves removed
2 litres boiling water
2 Campden tablets, crushed
1 tsp pectin enzyme
1.5 tsp citric acid
2.5 g red wine yeast
1.3 kg white sugar
250 g red grape concentrate
**Mature for:** 1 year
**Drink within:** 1 year

## Method

**1** Mash the elderberries and
blackberries in a plastic
bucket.
**2** Pour the boiling water over
the fruit and mix.
**3** Leave to cool to around 21°C
(70°F).
**4** Add a Campden tablet and
stir. Add the pectin enzyme
and citric acid. Stir well and
leave for 24 hours.
**5** Add the yeast and cover the
bucket. Over the next 5 days,
stir intermittently.
**6** Strain through a muslin.
**7** Add the sugar to the mixture
and stir well.
**8** Pour into a demijohn. Add
the red grape concentrate and
top up the volume to 4.5 litres
with water. Stir.
**9** Fit an airlock and store the
demijohn in a warm area
(20–22°C/68–72°F).
**10** When there are no more
bubbles passing through the
airlock add another Campden
tablet and syphon into a
demijohn with a fitted airlock.
**11** After 6 weeks the wine
should be clear and ready to
syphon into bottles.

# CLOVER WINE

## Ingredients

2 litres red clover flowers,
   stems removed
4.5 litres boiling water
1 kg white sugar
500 ml white grape juice
   (reconstituted from
   concentrate)
2 tsp acid blend
¼ tsp tannin
1 tsp yeast nutrient
2.5 g wine yeast
**Mature for:** 3 months
**Drink within:** 6 months

## Method

**1** Place the flowers in a
fermenting bin and pour over
some boiling water.
**2** Add the sugar, white grape
juice, acid blend, tannin and
yeast nutrient to the fermenter.
Top up the volume with 4.5
litres of boiling water.
**3** When the temperature is
lukewarm, pitch the yeast.

**4** Cover and leave to ferment
for 7 days.
**5** Strain the liquid into a
demijohn and fit an airlock.
Leave for 60 days.
**6** Syphon off and top up the
volume with water. Refit the
airlock and store for 4 months.
**7** Once bubbles stop
appearing in the airlock the
wine is clear. Leave for 10
days and then bottle.

### TWENTY-ONE-LEAF CLOVER

The world record for rare
clover formations was set in
2008, when a clover with
twenty one leaves was
discovered in the USA.

# HAW WINE

## Ingredients

2 kg hawthorn berries
4.5 litres boiling water
1 lemon
2 oranges
1 kg brown or white sugar
2.5 g wine yeast
1 tsp pectin enzyme
**Mature for:** 1 year
**Drink within:** 1 year

## Method

**1** Place the hawthorn berries in a large bowl and pour over enough boiling water to cover them. Leave for a week, stirring daily.
**2** Peel the rinds off the lemon and oranges and cut into thin strips. Squeeze the juice from the fruits. Place the rinds and juice into a bowl.
**3** Strain the berry liquid into the bowl.
**4** Cover the sugar in a little warm water and add to the bowl. Stir to ensure the sugar has dissolved.
**5** When the mixture has cooled, pitch the yeast and cover. Leave for 24 hours.
**6** Transfer to a fermentation jar and leave to ferment.
**7** If the wine doesn't clear, add pectin enzyme.

### HAWTHORN HABIT

During the World War I, soldiers smoked young hawthorn leaves in the absence of tobacco.

# LOGANBERRY WINE

## Ingredients

1.3 kg loganberries

1.3 kg white sugar

4.5 litres boiling water

1 tsp pectin enzyme

1 tsp citric acid

1 tsp yeast nutrient

2.5 g wine yeast

**Mature for:** 6 months

**Drink within:** 1 year

## Method

**1** Combine the loganberries and sugar in a fermenting bucket and cover with the boiling water. Stir to dissolve the sugar.

**2** When the mixture has cooled, add the pectin enzyme, citric acid, yeast nutrient and wine yeast and cover. Store for 7 days in a warm area, stirring daily.

**3** Strain into a demijohn with a fitted airlock and seal. Store in a warm area for a further 7 days to ferment.

**4** When the fermentation process has finished, rack off the wine into a jar and store in a cool place.

**5** When the wine has cleared, syphon into bottles and cork.

### ACCIDENTAL BERRY

The loganberry is a cross between a blackberry and a raspberry. It is believed it was accidentally developed in California by horticulturist James Harvey Logan in 1880 or 1881.

# PEAR WINE

## Ingredients

1.8 kg pears
4.5 litres boiling water
2 tsp pectin enzyme
900 g white sugar
juice of 2 lemons
2.5 g wine yeast
3 tsp yeast nutrient
1 Campden tablet, crushed
**Mature for:** 3 months
**Drink within:** 6 months

## Method

**1** Pour the boiling water over the pears and press down to extract as much juice from them as possible. Leave for 4–5 hours.
**2** Add the pectin enzyme and cover. Leave for 4 days to infuse.
**3** Strain through a muslin and pour the liquid into a demijohn.
**4** Add the sugar and lemon juice to the demijohn.
**5** Add the yeast and yeast nutrient and fit an airlock.
**6** Store in a warm room for 7–10 days.
**7** When the wine clears, syphon off, leaving the sediment behind.
**8** Store for another 3–4 days, and syphon off again into another demijohn. Add the Campden tablet.
**9** Seal the demijohn and store in a cool area for 10 days.
**10** Syphon into bottles and store in a cool area. Leave to mature for 3 months before tasting.

### PEAR TREE TITBIT

Pear trees can live for up to 300 years and grow to 18 m in height.

# POTATO WINE

## Ingredients

1.5 kg potatoes, washed and
    chopped, skin left on
water
1.5 kg demerara sugar
250 ml grape concentrate
250 ml cold black tea
1 tsp citric acid
2.5 g wine yeast
1 tsp yeast nutrient
2 Campden tablets, crushed
1 tsp potassium sorbate
**Mature for:** 3 months
**Drink within:** 6 months

## Method

**1** Boil the potatoes for 15 minutes, then strain through a muslin into a clean container.
**2** Add the sugar and stir.
**3** Once the sugar has dissolved, make up the volume with water to about 3.9 litres. Leave overnight.
**4** Add the grape concentrate, cold tea, citric acid, yeast and yeast nutrient, and stir well.
**5** Transfer the mixture to a demijohn, fit an airlock and leave until the frothing subsides. Top up with cold water if necessary.
**6** Monitor the airlock, and when the bubbles stop coming through, add 1 Campden tablet and the potassium sorbate and leave to clear.
**7** Syphon into a demijohn and store for 2 weeks.
**8** Add another Campden tablet before bottling.

### MR POTATO HEAD

American toy manufacturers Hasbro invented 'Mr Potato Head' in 1949. This was the first toy ever to be advertised on television appealing directly to children.

# ROSEHIP WINE

## Ingredients

1 kg rosehips, picked after the first frost
4.5 litres boiling water
1 kg white sugar
juice of 1 lemon
juice of 1 orange
2.5 g wine yeast
**Mature for:** 1 year
**Drink within:** 1 year

## Method

**1** Crush the rosehips and then place into a bucket of 4.5 litres of boiling water.
**2** Stir with a long-handled spoon and then store for 3 days, stirring intermittently.
**3** Strain the mixture.
**4** Make a syrup by mixing the sugar with the lemon and orange juice and add to the wine juice. Transfer the mixture to a fermentation jar and add the yeast.
**5** Fill the jar with boiled, cooled water, leaving a 3 cm gap at the top.
**6** Fit an airlock and leave to clear – about 3 months.
**7** Once cleared, syphon into a clean vessel and store for 3 months before bottling.

### ROSEHIP TIPS

• There are itchy hairs inside the hips, so wear gloves when handling them.
• Pick the ones that are vivid red and slightly soft, as they will have the best flavour.

### LEND A HAND ON THE LAND

In Britain during World War II, people were encouraged to pick wild rosehips and make a Vitamin C syrup for children, as many shipments containing citrus fruits were destroyed on their journey.

# ROWAN WINE

## Ingredients
1 kg rowanberries, stalks
  removed
2.85 litres boiling water
1.3 kg sugar
grated zest and juice of
  2 oranges
2.5 g wine yeast
**Mature for:** 6 months
**Drink within:** 1 year

## Method
**1** Put the rowanberries in a
bucket and pour 2 litres of
boiling water over them.
**2** Stir the liquid intermittently
for 3 days.
**3** Strain through a muslin into
a demijohn.
**4** Make a sugar syrup by
combining the sugar and
850 ml of boiling water and
add to the demijohn.
**5** Add the orange zest and
juice, and the yeast, to the
demijohn.

**6** Place a cotton-wool bung in
the demijohn and leave for
3 days.
**7** Fit an airlock and leave to
ferment for 4 months.
**8** Syphon into bottles and
store for 6 months before
consuming.

### URBAN LEGEND
According to Swedish folklore,
if rowan trees grew pale in
colour, it was a sign the local
population would suffer with
illnesses through the winter.

# SLOE WINE

## Ingredients

4.5 litres water

1.2 kg sloes

1 kg sugar

juice of 2 oranges

1 Campden tablet, crushed

2.5 g wine yeast

**Mature for**: 1 year

**Drink within**: 1 year

## Method

**1** Boil the sloes for 20 minutes in half the quantity of water.

**2** Crush them with a wooden spoon.

**3** Strain the pulp through some muslin to extract as much juice as possible. Pour the liquid into a plastic bucket.

**4** Boil the remaining water, add the sugar and stir until it has dissolved.

**5** Add the orange juice and Campden tablet.

**6** When the liquid has cooled, pitch the yeast, cover, and leave to ferment for 4 days.

**7** After 4 days, transfer wort to a fermentation container and store for 3 months. After this time the wine should have cleared.

**8** Transfer to bottles and store for at least a year before drinking to get the best results from this wine.

### SLOE PRESERVES

The leftover berries discarded when sieving can be made into jam, jelly or chutney. See page 139 for the sloe gin recipe.

### READY, SET, SLOE!

Blackthorn bushes bear their white blossom early in spring when hedgerows are still bare, so they are easy to identify.

# PART 5

# WINTER

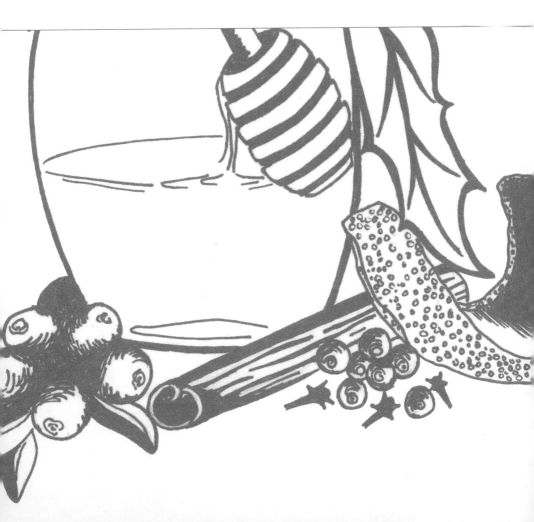

# BREWING IN WINTER

ന്ദന

Even though the days are at their shortest and darkest and the weather is at its coldest, don't let that deter you from getting out there and foraging for another season's worth of ingredients.

Winter is an exciting time with the Christmas holiday and the end of one year and start of another. The warming beers, ciders, and seasonal wines in this section are perfectly suited to surviving the winter chill. There is a long tradition of strong beers being brewed in cold countries for the winter, and even in the days of central heating we still crave these warming drinks. Wholesome meals and comfort food are also on the menu, so be sure to check tho rccipe section (pages 121–131) for winter favourites. The recipes included use drinks you've brewed throughout the year, making the most of your creations. Before you get started, remember to sanitize all your equipment and do your usual bottle checks.

## BEER

Strong ales, malty flavours and fruity and spicy beers are in demand during this season. Besides the warming effect, there is a lot to celebrate and beer certainly makes you feel festive. You'll find lots of seasonal ales in the pubs and shops – even the established beer and lager manufacturers bring out their own Christmas-themed drinks during the winter. Brewing your own beer is more fun, however, as you have ultimate control over the finished product.

Christmas ale (page 108) is a

richly flavoured brew packed full of festive flavours. Cinnamon, nutmeg, cloves, orange, ginger, honey and chocolate represent the tastes and smells of Christmas. This ale is sure to get you in the mood for the holiday.

English old ale (page 109) is a traditional drink that's been brewed in the United Kingdom for centuries. It is characteristically dark in colour and has strong, malty flavours. The alcohol content can range from 6.0% ABV to 8.0% ABV so it will definitely keep you warm on a cold night.

Maple porter is a variation on the porter style. The name 'porter' comes from its popularity among street and river porters in 18th-century London. Today, porters are popular all over the world and are available with flavours such as honey, bourbon, vanilla and pumpkin. The recipe on page 110 creates a dark and full-bodied beer

which is made sweeter with the addition of maple syrup.

Schwarzbier means 'black beer' in German and this beverage is just that: black. Schwarzbier shares some flavours with stouts and porters but is slightly more bitter. It's also similar in appearance to a stout, with its dark body and thick white head. See the recipe on page 111.

Spiced honey beer (page 112) is a complex, wheaty and hoppy version of the spiced cider recipes that follow in this section. Less fruity than its cider counterparts, spiced honey beer has a mead edge, with the sweet honey flavour bursting through the savoury.

## CIDER

The ciders that are popular during this season tend to be served warm and packed full of interesting flavours. Where mulled wine is perhaps more traditional during the winter, mulled cider (page 113) is also a popular winter beverage.

Cinnamon (*Cinnamomum verum*) is in most mulled drink recipes and as well as providing flavour, it has antioxidant properties. It is said to relieve digestive problems, toothache and common colds.

Also to be found in most mulled drinks recipes are cloves, the dried flower buds of the tree *Syzygium aromaticum*. They are also noted for their health benefits and are used for pain relief in Chinese and Indian medicine, and in Western herbalism and dentistry. Chinese medicine notes the ability of cloves to warm the stomach, which may be why they feature so often in mulled drink recipes.

The combination of fruit, spice and warmth is a healthy one and has been known for its medicinal properties for centuries. Hot spiced honey cider (page 114) is a delicious variation on the classic mulled cider recipe. Honey is another ingredient famous for its healthy properties. A glass of hot spiced honey cider will soothe a sore throat and cheer you up in the process!

**MEAD AND COUNTRY WINES**
Melomel mead (page 115) is a Christmas drink flavoured with cranberries and orange peel. Cranberries have connections with Christmas and feature strongly in the American holiday of Thanksgiving, which also takes place during the winter season. Cranberries are usually commercially farmed, but it is possible to grow them in a windowbox or in your garden. They need a moderate climate and acidic soil. While harvesting your cranberries, pick enough for the cranberry wine recipe on page (117) as well as for melomel mead.

Cranberries have gained the commercial status of 'superfruit' on account of their high nutritional content and antioxidant properties. They are also consumed as a dried fruit or made into preserves such as cranberry sauce, the traditional accompaniment to your Christmas day roast.

The expression 'crabby', often applied to a bad-tempered person, is derived from the sourness of the crab apple (*Malus sylvestris*). In the recipe for crab apple wine (page 116), the sour flavour is balanced out by cooking apples, resulting in a much more palatable wine. As well as wine, crab apples make an excellent jam when they are chopped up and combined with hedgerow favourites such as sloes, rowanberries, elderberries, rosehips or hawthorn berries.

The parsnip (*Pastinaca sativa*) is a favourite winter vegetable which is more than likely to make an appearance at the Christmas Day meal. There is a good deal of sugar in parsnips, so this vegetable creates a very sweet wine.

Dig them up as late in the season as possible – they benefit from staying in the ground while it is cold, as this develops their flavour. See page 118 for the recipe.

Perhaps the most traditional of all Christmas and winter drinks is Wassail wine (page 119). It is a hot and spicy drink, similar to mulled cider, except that this recipe uses a higher quantity of dried fruit and mixed spices. Among the traditional cinnamon and nutmeg are added oranges, tangerine zest and mace. The warming spices and fruity aroma of this drink makes it a perfect winter warmer that really feels like Christmas in a glass.

The final section of the book (pages 133–139) includes recipes for cocktails, liqueurs and infusions. These combine shop-bought spirits and liqueurs with your own home brews and hedgerow fruits.

# CHRISTMAS ALE

## Ingredients

225 g crystal malt 80 L
225 g chocolate malt
225 g black patent malt
20 litres unchlorinated water
900 g dry dark malt extract
1.3 kg clover honey
60 g Northern Brewer hops
30 g Cascade hops
¼ tsp Irish moss
3 oranges, peeled, in
    segments
3 cinnamon sticks
2 whole nutmegs
6 whole cloves
30 g root ginger, grated
1 vial White Labs Irish ale
    yeast
200 g dry malt extract, for
    bottle conditioning
**Mature for:** 1 week
**Drink within:** 1 year

## Method

**1** Combine the crystal malt, chocolate malt and black patent malt in the unchlorinated water and steep at 70°C (158°F) for 30 minutes.

**2** Remove the grains and add the dry dark malt extract, clover honey and Northern Brewer hops. Boil for 30 minutes.

**3** Twenty-five minutes in to the boil, add the Cascade hops and Irish moss.

**4** Turn off the heat and add the oranges, spices and ginger.

**5** Allow to steep for 30 minutes, then strain.

**6** Cool the wort and pitch the yeast.

**7** Allow to ferment for 1 week and then transfer to a secondary fermenting bin.

**8** Ferment for a further 5 days.

**9** Bulk prime with 200g of dry malt extract then bottle.

# ENGLISH OLD ALE

## Ingredients

3 kg dark liquid malt extract

250 g corn sugar

300 ml molasses

45 g Czech Saaz hop pellets

water

¼ tsp Irish moss

11 g English ale yeast

60 g cane sugar, for bottle
    conditioning

**Mature for**: 2 months

**Drink within**: 6 months

## Method

**1** Combine the malt extract,
corn sugar, molasses and 30 g
hop pellets and cover with 6
litres of boiling water. Leave to
boil for 15 minutes.

**2** Add the Irish moss and boil
for a further 10 minutes.

**3** Take off the heat and add
the remaining hops. Steep for
2 minutes.

**4** Pour 8 litres of pre-boiled
cold water into the fermenting
vessel and then strain the
wort into the vessel.

**5** Top up the volume to 19 litres
and pitch the yeast.

**6** Fit an airlock and store in a
warm, dark area for 2 weeks:
primary fermentation should
take 1 week, secondary
fermentation should take
another week.

**7** Bulk prime with 60 g of cane
sugar and then bottle.

**MEDICINAL ALE**

A folk remedy for constipation
was old ale with the pounded
root of *Iris foetidissima*.

# MAPLE PORTER

tɔʊɔ

## Ingredients

700 g crystal malt 60 L

225 g black patent malt

water

2.5 kg light dry malt extract

70 g Goldings hop pellets

450 g maple syrup

11 g ale yeast

100 g cane sugar for bottle
    conditioning

**Mature for:** 2 months

**Drink within:** 6 months

## Method

**1** Crush the malts and place
them in a sparge bag, inside a
large containter.

**2** Steep for 15 minutes in 10
litres of cold water.

**3** Heat the water to 75°C (167°F).

**4** Remove the sparge bag and
hold it over the pot, allowing
the liquid to flow out of it.

**5** Bring the liquid to a boil and
add the light dry malt extract
and 30 g Goldings hop pellets.
Boil for 60 minutes.

**6** Thirty minutes in to the boil,
add 30 g Goldings hop pellets.

**7** Forty-five minutes in to the
boil, add the maple syrup and
the remaining 10 g Goldings
hop pellets.

**8** When the 60 minutes is up,
cool the wort to fermentation
temperature of 21°C (70°F).

**9** Transfer to a fermenting bin,
top up the volume to 23 litres
and add the yeast. Store for
5–7 days.

**10** Rack off to a secondary
fermenting bin for a further
7 days.

**11** When fermentation is
complete, bulk prime with
100 g of cane sugar and bottle.

### SWEET TREAT

Maple syrup is very high in
calories, but contains zinc,
potassium, magnesium,
calcium, iron and manganese.

# SCHWARZBIER

ཉཉ

## Ingredients

water

120 g dextrine malt

230 g caraMunich malt

120 g chocolate malt

60 g black patent malt

1.5 kg liquid light malt extract

1.3 kg light dry malt extract

28 g Northern Brewer hops

28 g Hallertauer Hersbrucker
  hops

1 tsp Irish moss

11 g lager yeast

110 g cane sugar, for bottle
  conditioning

**Mature for:** 2 months

**Drink within:** 6 months

## Method

**1** Heat 8 litres of water to 75°C (167°F) and add the grains. Steep for 60 minutes.

**2** Rinse through the grains with 4 litres of water at the same temperature.

**3** Bring the liquid to a boil and add the malt extracts and the Northern Brewer hops. Let the liquid boil for 60 minutes.

**4** Forty-five minutes in to the boil, add the Hallertauer hops.

**5** Fifty-five minutes in to the boil, add the Irish moss.

**6** Once the 60 minutes are up, turn off the heat.

**7** Remove the hops and transfer to a fermenting bin. Top up with water to 19 litres.

**8** Check the temperature of the wort and when it cools to 21°C (70°F), pitch the yeast.

**9** Ferment for 1 week at 16°C (61°F).

**10** Transfer to a secondary fermenting bin and ferment for 3 weeks at 10°C (50°F).

**11** Bulk prime with 110 g of cane sugar prior to bottling.

**12** Store the bottles for 1 week at room temperature and then move to a cooler area (5°C/41°F) to mature.

# SPICED HONEY BEER

## Ingredients

water

2.5 kg liquid light malt extract

900 g honey

90 g Hallertauer hops

35 g crushed coriander seeds

14 g dried orange peel

11 g wheat beer yeast

120 g cane sugar, for bottle
 conditioning

**Mature for:** 2 weeks

**Drink within:** 6 months

## Method

**1** Boil 7.5 litres of water and
add the malt extract, honey
and 60 g Hallertauer hops.

**2** Forty-five minutes in to the
boil, add a further 15 g hops
and 20 g crushed coriander.
Boil for a further 10 minutes.

**3** Add the remaining
coriander and orange peel
and boil for 5 minutes.

**4** Add the remaining hops
and boil for a further 2
minutes.

**5** Pour 8 litres of water into the
fermenting bin.

**6** Strain the boiled liquid and
add to the fermenting bin.

**7** Top up the volume to 23 litres
and add the yeast.

**8** Cover the fermenting bin
with a tea towel and loosely
place the bin's lid over it.

**9** Store in a warm, dark area
to ferment for 2 weeks.

**10** When fermentation is
complete, bulk prime with
120 g cane sugar.

**11** Bottle and store for 2 weeks.

---

### TIPPLER'S TIP

Leave out the coriander seeds
if you wish to create a sweet
and not-so-spicy honey beer.

# MULLED CIDER

## Ingredients

2.2 litres still, dry home-
   brewed cider (see page 39)
3 apples, cored and sliced
2 oranges, sliced
8 whole cloves
juice and zest of 1 lemon
2 tsp ground mixed spices
6 tbsp light soft brown sugar
2 cinnamon sticks, about 4 cm
   each
**Mature for:** Serve
immediately
**Drink within:** 1 year

## Method

**1** Combine all the ingredients
together in a saucepan and
heat gently but do not allow
to boil.
**2** Stir the mixture as it heats
through for a minimum of
1 hour.
**3** Strain into cups when ready.

### WINTER WARMER

Mulled beverages such as this
can be made in advance of
the holiday season and
stored; the spices will
preserve the drink. Transfer
the liquid to an airtight
container and store in a cool,
dark area such as a
cupboard.

# HOT SPICED HONEY CIDER

### Ingredients

1 litre still, scrumpy cider (see page 39)
4 tbsp honey
peel of 1 orange
2 cinnamon sticks
2 tsp ground allspice
**Mature for:** Serve immediately
**Drink within:** 1 year

### Method

**1** Combine all the ingredients together in a saucepan and heat gently but do not allow to boil.
**2** Stir the mixture for 15 minutes.
**3** When the mixture has warmed through, strain into cups.

### SPICE IT UP!

Adding a small handful of whole cloves will make this drink even more spicy.

### CINNAMON BONUS

Cinnamon contains a high quantity of powerful antioxidants.

# MELOMEL MEAD

## Ingredients

3 kg honey

3 litres unchlorinated water

700 g fresh cranberries

zest of 2 oranges

6 tsp pectin enzyme

6 tsp yeast nutrient

2.5 g wine yeast

**Mature for:** 1 year

**Drink within:** 1 year

## Method

**1** Put the honey in 2 litres of water, bring to the boil and add the cranberries. Remove from the heat when the cranberries go 'pop' and become translucent.

**2** Add the orange zest, pectin enzyme and yeast nutrient. Leave to cool.

**3** Take out the orange zest and transfer the mixture to a demijohn.

**4** Add the yeast, seal with a bung and fit an airlock. Store in a warm area.

**5** The airlock should start bubbling and foam will form on the top of the liquid. Store for 2 weeks and monitor the bubbles, which should begin to slow down.

**6** When the sediment is 2–3 cm thick, rack off to a secondary fermenting bin.

**7** Top up with fresh water and refit the bung and airlock, exposing the mead to as little oxygen as possible.

**8** Check the mead daily and repeat the racking process as the sediment builds up again. Top up as necessary. When the bubbling has ceased the fermentation is complete. Syphon into bottles.

## ANCIENT ALCOHOL

Mead is the oldest fermented beverage in history, dating back 8,000 years.

# CRAB APPLE WINE

## Ingredients

1 kg crab apples
225 g cooking apples
water
1.2 kg white sugar
zest and juice of 1 orange
zest and juice of 1 lemon
2.5 g wine yeast
**Mature for:** 1 year
**Drink within:** 1 year

## Method

**1** Crush the apples into a plastic bucket.
**2** Pour 2 litres of boiling water over them and leave to cool down.
**3** Mash and then, over the next 3 days, stir intermittently.
**4** Strain through a wine bag into a 4.5 litre demijohn.
**5** Make a syrup with 800 ml of water and 1.2 kg of sugar. Pour into the demijohn.
**6** Add the orange and lemon zest and juice to the demijohn.
**7** Pitch the yeast.
**8** Top up the liquid to 4.5 litres with pre-boiled, cooled water.
**9** Leave the wine to ferment for 4 months.
**10** Syphon into a clean 4.5 litre demijohn and store for 3 months before bottling.

### APPLE AND BLACKCURRANT

For a variation on this recipe, substitute the cooking apples with 450 g blackcurrants.

# CRANBERRY WINE

𝕊𝕒

## Ingredients

2 kg cranberries, chopped
450 g raisins, chopped
1 kg granulated sugar
4 litres boiling water
½ tsp pectin enzyme
1 tsp yeast nutrient
2.5 g champagne yeast
**Mature for:** 6–8 months
**Drink within:** 1 year

## Method

**1** Combine the cranberries and raisins and pour the sugar over them. Transfer to a bucket.
**2** Add the boiling water and leave to cool.
**3** Once at room temperature, add the pectin enzyme and yeast nutrient. Stir and cover. Set to one side for 12 hours.
**4** Add the yeast and re-cover.
**5** Store again for 14 days, stirring daily.
**6** After the 14 days, strain through a muslin.
**7** Transfer to a fermenting bin and fit an airlock.
**8** After 30 days, top up with water and refit the airlock.
**9** Rack into bottles and age for 6–8 months.

# PARSNIP WINE

ಬಲ

## Ingredients

226 g raisins
4.5 litres water
1.8 kg parsnips, skins on
1.3 kg white sugar
zest and juice of 1 lemon
1 tsp pectin enzyme
1 Campden tablet, crushed
2.5 g wine yeast
1 tsp yeast nutrient
**Mature for:** 6 months
**Drink within:** 1 year

## Method

**1** First, rinse the raisins in some hot water to remove the wax on the skin. When they have cooled, chop them.
**2** Place the raisins in a pan, cover with water and simmer for 5 minutes. Strain through a muslin and put to one side.
**3** Scrub the parsnips, slice thinly and place in a large saucepan. Cover the parsnips with water, bring to the boil and cook until tender – about 10 minutes.
**4** Take the pan off the heat and allow the contents to cool. Strain off the liquid and return it to the pan, discarding the parsnips.
**5** Add the sugar and lemon zest and juice. Simmer for 45 minutes, stirring intermittently.
**6** Strain the mixture into a plastic bucket and allow to cool to a lukewarm temperature.
**7** Add the pectin enzyme and Campden tablet. Store for 24 hours in a warm area.
**8** Stir in the yeast and yeast nutrient and cover. Store for 4 days in a warm area, stirring daily.
**9** Strain into a fermentation jar and fit an airlock. Leave the wine to clear.
**10** Syphon and bottle once cleared.

# WASSAIL WINE

## Ingredients

muslin bag of mixed spices:
   cinnamon sticks, whole
   allspice, lightly crushed,
   mace, shavings of nutmeg
   and 2 cloves
3 litres boiling water
2 large oranges, chopped
grated zest of 2 tangerines
1.3 kg mixed dried fruit
1 tsp pectin enzyme
1 tsp citric acid
1.1 kg white sugar
2.5 g wine yeast
1 tsp yeast nutrient
1 litre red grape concentrate
**Mature for:** 2 weeks
**Drink within:** 1 year

## Method

**1** Place the spice bag in the boiling water and simmer for a few minutes.

**2** Add the oranges, tangerine zest and mixed dried fruit to the boiling water and simmer for 10 minutes.

**3** Remove from the heat and pour into a fermenting bin.

**4** Add the pectin enzyme and citric acid and leave overnight.

**5** Retrieve the orange pieces from the mixture and squeeze to extract all the juice. Discard the orange pieces.

**6** Repeat this process with the mixed dried fruit.

**7** Dissolve the sugar in some hot water. When cooled, add to the fermenting bin.

**8** Add the yeast, yeast nutrient and red grape concentrate to the fermenting bin. Stir.

**9** Leave the wine to ferment for 5 days, stirring daily.

**10** Strain through a muslin into a demijohn and fit an airlock.

**11** When fermentation has ceased, syphon into bottles.

# PART 6

# COMPANION FOOD RECIPES

Home-brews don't only have to be for drinking – incorporating them into your cooking adds another dimension to your hobby. Over the next few pages you'll find recipes selected to make the most of your creations.

# Amuse-bouche of Almonds and Blue Cheese with Cherries Soaked in Cherry Wine

## Ingredients – Serves 8
8 cherries, stones removed and sliced in half
250 ml home-brewed cherry wine (see page 68)
zest of 1 lemon
2 tsp sugar
Stilton cheese
honeycomb
4 almonds, sliced in half

## Method
**1** Soak the cherries in enough cherry wine to cover them for an hour.
**2** Put the remaining wine, the lemon zest and the sugar in a pan and bring to the boil. Reduce the heat and add the soaked cherries to the pan. Allow them to poach for 1 minute.
**3** Remove the pan from the heat and leave the cherries soaking for 30 minutes. When cold, refrigerate.
**4** Roll 8 pieces of stilton into the size of cherry stones.
**5** Place a piece of stilton between two cherry halves. Arrange carefully on a spoon.
**6** Position a small piece of honeycomb and an almond slice next to the cherries.
**7** Serve as a bite-sized treat.

# Apple Fritters in Perry Batter with Perry Syrup

**Ingredients – Serves 6**

*Syrup*

150 ml dry or semi-dry home-
  brewed perry (see page 40)
juice of 1 lemon
100 g caster sugar

*Batter*

140 g plain flour
pinch of salt
1 tsp cinnamon
2 drops vanilla essence
1 medium egg, separated
250 ml dry or semi-dry home-
  brewed perry
sunflower oil
4 apples, peeled, cored and
  sliced to 1 cm thick

**Method**

**1** Make the syrup by heating the home-brewed perry, lemon juice and caster sugar together. Stir until the sugar has dissolved. Bring to the boil and then simmer for 5 minutes. Transfer the syrup to a jug and allow to cool.

**2** Make the batter by sifting the flour into a bowl. Add a pinch of salt, teaspoon of cinnamon and drops of vanilla essence. Make a well in the flour and drop in the egg yolk and one third of the perry.

**3** Whisk the ingredients, adding more perry until a smooth batter is formed. Set aside for 30 minutes.

**4** Whisk the egg white until it forms soft peaks, then fold into the batter.

**5** Pour some oil into a frying pan and heat. Dry the apple slices and dip into the batter.

**6** Place in the frying pan and cook until they are golden brown and puffed.

**7** Remove from the pan and dab with kitchen paper to remove any grease.

**8** Serve with a splash of perry syrup and a dollop of vanilla ice cream.

# Beer and Two-Cheese Bread

## Ingredients – Makes 2 loaves

450 ml home-brewed nut
   brown ale, at room
   temperature (see page 84)
4 tsp sugar
2 tsp dried yeast
520 g strong white bread flour
320 g wholemeal flour
200 g Cheddar cheese, grated
75 g Parmesan cheese, grated
50 g milk powder
1½ tsp salt
2 eggs, beaten
1 egg, white only

## Method

**1** Pour the nut brown ale into
a bowl and add the sugar and
yeast. Set aside.
**2** In a larger bowl, combine
the flours, cheeses, milk, salt
and beaten eggs.
**3** Pour the home-brewed nut
brown ale and yeast mixture
into the larger bowl.

**4** Mix until a soft dough forms.
Knead the dough until the
consistency becomes smooth.
**5** Divide the dough into 2
portions and place on baking
trays.
**6** Score the loaves and cover
with a damp tea towel. Set
aside somewhere warm
and dry.
**7** When the dough has risen,
pre-heat the oven to 200°C
(400°F/Gas mark 6).
**8** Brush each loaf with the egg
white. Bake the loaves in the
oven for 25–30 minutes, until
golden and cooked through.

# Beer-battered Haddock and Chips

**Ingredients – Serves 4**

225 g self-raising flour

salt and pepper

300 ml home-brewed beer or
    lager (see page 62 or 64)

beef dripping, sunflower
    oil or vegetable oil for
    deep frying

6–8 large potatoes for chips

4 thick haddock fillets

**Method**

**1** Prepare the batter for the
fish by sifting the flour and a
pinch of salt into a bowl.
Whisk in the beer or lager. A
thick batter consistency
should develop. If the mixture
seems too thick, add another
splash of beer or lager.

**2** Preheat the oven to 150°C
(300°F/Gas mark 2).

**3** Peel the potatoes, cut into
chips and wash. Preheat the
dripping or oil to 120°C (250°F)
in a deep heavy-based
saucepan or deep fat fryer.

**4** Place the chips in a mesh
basket, lower into the fat and
fry for 8–10 minutes.

**5** Once they are cooked, lift
them out of the pan and leave
to cool slightly on greaseproof
paper.

**6** Heat the fat to 180°C (350°F).

**7** Season the fish with salt and
pepper and dust lightly with
flour. Coat the fish in the beer
or lager batter. Remember
that the fat is very hot, so
place the fish in the pan
carefully and fry for 8–10
minutes until golden and
crispy.

**10** Remove the fish from the
pan, lay on greaseproof paper
and place in the oven to keep
warm.

**11** Return the chips to the pan
for 2–3 minutes, or until they
are brown and crisp.

# Belly of Pork in Cider

## Ingredients - Serves 4

1 kg pork belly

salt and pepper

2 tbsp olive oil

2 large onions, finely chopped

2 garlic cloves, crushed

250 g button mushrooms, sliced.

500 ml sparkling dry cider (see page 87)

2 leeks, chopped

2 carrots, chopped

1 small cabbage, chopped

800 g potatoes, peeled and cut into chunks

## Method

**1** Preheat the oven to 150°C (300°F/Gas mark 2).

**2** Season the pork with salt and pepper, roll it and tie it with kitchen string.

**3** Heat the olive oil in a frying pan and add the onions, garlic and mushrooms. Fry over a medium heat until the onions start to brown.

**4** Add the pork and fry until browned on all sides.

**5** Transfer the contents of the frying pan to a large pan. Pour the cider over and season with salt and pepper. Simmer for 1 hour.

**6** Add the vegetables to the pan and simmer for a further 30 minutes.

**7** Meanwhile, cook the potatoes in boiling salted water for about 15 minutes. When they are tender, drain and mash them.

**8** At the end of the cooking time, remove the pork from the pan and cut off the string. Slice the pork into chunks and place on a bed of mashed potato. Spoon the vegetables around the pork and finish by drizzling the cider gravy over the dish.

# Duck Breast in Plum Wine Sauce

### Ingredients – Serves 1

1 boneless duck breast, with
  skin on
1 tsp five-spice powder
1 tbsp fresh root ginger, finely
  chopped
3 spring onions, white part
  only, finely chopped
50 ml clear honey
pinch of salt and pepper
120 ml sesame oil
150 ml home-brewed plum
  wine (see page 74)
400 ml duck stock
28 g unsalted butter

### Method

**1** Marinate the duck in the spices, ginger, spring onions, honey, salt, pepper and sesame oil for a minimum of 6 hours.
**2** Preheat the oven to 180°C (350°F/Gas mark 4).
**3** Heat a frying pan and sear the duck breast until browned all over, skin side down first to release some fat.
**4** Transfer the duck to the oven for 10 minutes to cook it to medium rare.
**5** Pour the grease from the frying pan and discard.
**6** Add the home-brewed plum wine and duck stock to the frying pan and reduce the sauce down. Season with salt and pepper.
**7** Add the butter to the sauce and stir it in. Place to one side and keep warm.
**8** Remove the duck from the oven and let it rest for 5 minutes before slicing.
**9** Pour the plum wine sauce over the duck and serve.

---

**TASTY TIP**

Serve with a good Shiraz or Valpolicella.

---

# Poached Pears in Blackberry Wine

## Ingredients – Serves 6

6–12 ripe pears, depending on
size (Conference or William
work nicely)
juice of ½ lemon
750 ml water
400 ml home-brewed
blackberry wine (see
page 92)
200 g sugar
55 g honey
1 vanilla pod, split
1 strip of lemon rind
cream or ice cream, to serve

## Method

**1** Peel the pears, leaving the
stems attached. Sprinkle
lemon juice over them to
prevent them going brown.
**2** Remove the core from the
pears with an apple corer,
keeping the pears whole.
**3** Put the water, home-brewed
blackberry wine, sugar,
honey, vanilla pod and
lemon rind in a large pan
over a medium heat. Stir to
dissolve the sugar and bring
to the boil.
**4** Add the pears and poach for
5–10 minutes.
**5** When the pears are tender,
carefully lift them out of the
pan and set to one side.
**6** Boil the liquid in the pan
until it thickens to a syrup.
**7** Spoon the syrup over
poached pears and serve the
with cream or ice cream.

# Sausages with Cider and Apple

### Ingredients – Serves 4

1 tbsp oil

8 pork sausages

4 large onions, peeled and cut
into rough chunks

1 tsp English mustard

a pinch of thyme

1 bay leaf

250 ml home-brewed sweet
cider (see page 88)

salt and pepper

1 large red dessert apple,
cored but not peeled

### Method

**1** Heat the oil in a pan. Prick the sausages with a fork and fry until browned.

**2** Add the onions to the pan and allow them to brown slightly.

**3** Stir in the mustard, thyme, bay leaf and home-brewed cider.

**4** Cover and simmer gently for 30 minutes.

**5** After 30 minutes the liquid in the pan should resemble a gravy. Season with salt and pepper as desired.

**6** Divide the apple into 8–10 slices and arrange over the contents of the pan. Cover and simmer for 5 minutes. The apples should soften but retain their original shape.

**7** This dish is best served with a sweet potato mash. Place the sausages and apple slices on top of the mash and cover with cider gravy. Add some grainy mustard to your mash for an extra kick.

## BANGERS'N'MASH

Sausages and mashed potato are known as 'bangers and mash' in Britain. Some sources attribute this to the poor-quality sausages available during World War II, which would often explode if cooked on a very high heat.

# Stout-soaked Beef Burgers

## Ingredients – Serves 4

450 g minced beef
200 ml Irish stout (see page 37)
4 garlic cloves, crushed
1 onion, very finely chopped
salt and pepper
1 tbsp olive oil
4 mozzarella slices (optional)

## Method

**1** Put the beef in a bowl and pour over enough Irish stout to cover it. Cover the bowl with clingfilm and place in the fridge. Leave for 1 hour.
**2** After the 1 hour is up, take the bowl out of the fridge and pour away any stout that hasn't absorbed into the meat.
**3** Add the crushed garlic and chopped onion to the bowl and mix into the beef, using a fork.
**4** Once the mixture has a smooth consistency, take chunks in your hands and mould into burger-sized shapes.
**5** Heat the olive oil in a frying pan and add the burgers. Fry on a moderate heat until cooked through. If you want to make cheeseburgers, top each burger with a slice of mozzarella just before you take them off the heat.
**6** Serve the classic way – in a bun and with a side of chips.

Stout can be used in a variety of other dishes, working particularly well as an ingredient in gravy. Try the following suggestions to make the best of your home-brew:

• *Braised Beef and Ale Stew with Horseradish Dumplings*
• *Irish Stout Chicken Stew*
• *Shepherd's Pie*
• *Steak and Ale Pie*
• *Sticky Pork Ribs in BBQ and Beer Sauce*
• *Stout Soup.*

# Strawberry Wine Jelly

### Ingredients – Serves 6
500 g strawberries
300 ml strawberry wine (see page 75)
110 g caster sugar
210 ml water
11 g powdered gelatin

### Method
**1** Wash and hull the strawberries. Put six to one side for decoration later. Pulp the remaining strawberries in a blender and then sieve to remove all the seeds.
**2** Put the wine, sugar and 150 ml of water in a pan and bring to the boil. Stir until you have a syrup-like consistency.
**3** Pour the syrup mixture over the strawberries and leave for 30 minutes.
**4** Place 60 ml of cold water into a dish and add the gelatin. Leave for 5 minutes.
**5** Return the strawberry syrup mixture to the pan. Add the gelatin and water and simmer. Stir until the gelatin is dissolved and do not allow the mixture to boil.
**6** Pour into jelly moulds and place in the refrigerator to set.
**7** When the jelly is set, top with the whole strawberries you kept to one side earlier.

This recipe works just as well using:

• blackberries and blackberry wine
• crab apples and crab apple wine
• cranberries and cranberry wine
• loganberries and loganberry wine

Strawberry wine can also be used as a basis for a fruit salad or thickened with strained strawberries and turned into a coulis.

# PART 7

# COCKTAILS, LIQUEURS AND INFUSIONS

Cocktails and infusions are always popular and make parties and celebrations more fun and special. The following recipes use commercially produced spirits or liqueurs or drinks that you've home-brewed – or sometimes both together. The best thing about cocktails is how adaptable they are. Play around with the recipes given here, substitute ingredients and create your own signature cocktails. Infusing spirits is a longer process but just as rewarding once you've discovered a winning recipe.

# APPLE CIDER COCKTAIL

## Ingredients
60 ml home-brewed turbo
    cider (see page 65)
30 ml vodka
15 ml melon liqueur
ice cubes
1 splash sweet and sour mix
1 apple slice

## Method
**1** Combine the cider, vodka and melon liqueur in a cocktail shaker filled with crushed ice.
**2** Shake vigorously.
**3** Strain into a chilled Martini glass.
**4** Add a splash of sweet and sour mix.
**5** Garnish with a slice of apple.

### APPLE LIQUEUR
You can substitute apple liqueur for the melon liqueur to reinforce the apple flavour in this cocktail, if you prefer.

# BLACKBERRY BRANDY

### Ingredients
500 g blackberries
225 g caster sugar
1 litre brandy

### Method
**1** Place the blackberries in a large jar with an airtight lid.
**2** Add the sugar and brandy.
**3** Seal the jar tightly and shake vigorously.
**4** Store in a cool, dark cupboard for 9 weeks. For the first week, shake the jar every other day. For the next 8 weeks, shake the jar once a week.
**5** Strain off into a bottle and enjoy!

# BLACKCURRANT GIN

### Ingredients
100 g blackcurrants
6 tsp caster sugar
750 ml gin

### Method
**1** Prepare the blackcurrants by pricking them with a fork, which will help to bring out their flavour later.
**2** Put the blackcurrants and sugar in a jar and cover with the gin.
**3** Seal the jar and shake vigorously.
**4** Store for 2 weeks, shaking occasionally.
**5** Strain the gin through a sieve and bottle.

# CHERRY BRANDY

### Ingredients
900 g Morello cherries, stoned
170 g cane sugar
400 ml brandy

### Method
**1** Set out some sterilized glass bottles and distribute the cherries among them, sprinkling the sugar between the cherries as they are dropped in.

**2** Pour the brandy into each bottle, leaving a gap at the neck.

**3** Seal the bottles and store in a cupboard.

**4** Leave for 2–3 months before drinking.

# CIDER WITH CALVADOS

### Ingredients
1 part Calvados
9 parts home-brewed sparkling dry cider (see page 87)
Angostura bitters
1 small sugar cube
Maraschino cherry
slice of orange

### Method
**1** Pour the Calvados into a chilled champagne flute and top up with home-brewed cider.

**2** Add a dash of Angostura bitters over the sugar cube.

**3** Garnish with a cherry and a slice of orange.

# GORSE AND STRAWBERRY BELLINI

## Ingredients
100 g strawberries, hulled
2 tbsp caster sugar
home-brewed gorse wine (see
    page 49)
splash of Prosecco

## Method
**1** Blend the strawberries and sugar together to make a purée consistency.
**2** Measure the quantity of the purée. Add double the amount of home-brewed gorse wine to the mixture and stir well.
**3** Top up with a splash of Prosecco.
**4** Pour into a chilled champagne glass. Enjoy!

### SALUTE!
Bellinis were invented in the famous Harry's Bar in Venice, a favourite haunt of celebrities.

# LAVENDER-INFUSED VODKA

## Ingredients
1 sprig of rosemary
2 sprigs of lavender
750 ml vodka

## Method
**1** Place the herbs in a jar with an airtight lid.
**2** Pour the vodka into the jar, seal tightly and shake.
**3** Store the jar in a dark area such as a cupboard for 5 days.
**4** Try the mixture every day after the second day, until the mixture is to your liking. Then strain the herbs out using a strainer or coffee filter.
**5** Wash the jar and return the strained vodka to it.
**6** Store in the fridge or freezer.

# HEDGEROW PORT

## Ingredients
1 kg elderberries
250 g blackcurrants
525 g blackberries
525 g raisins
1.2 kg sugar
1 tsp tartaric acid
½ tsp port yeast and nutrient
1 tsp pectin enzyme
water

## Method
**1** Remove the stalks from the berries and rinse the berries in cold water.
**2** Place the berries and raisins in a large plastic container.
**3** Boil enough water to fill the container and cover the berries. Leave to stand for 24 hours.
**4** Strain the mixture through muslin into a pan. Discard the berries.
**5** Add the sugar and tartaric acid to the pan and simmer for an hour, ensuring that the sugar dissolves.
**6** When the mixture cools to a lukewarm temperature add the yeast, yeast nutrient and pectin enzyme. Stir well.
**7** Pour the mixture into a fermentation jar and fit an airlock. Top up with water and store in a dark area for 2 weeks.
**8** Syphon into another vessel and then syphon into bottles.
**9** Leave in a dark place to mature for at least 2 weeks.

# HEDGEROW SLING

## Ingredients
50 ml home-brewed sloe gin (see below)
25 ml lemon juice
crushed ice
soda
12 ml blackberry liqueur
a few blackberries

## Method
1 Combine the home-brewed sloe gin with lemon juice and some crushed ice in a cocktail shaker.
2 Shake vigorously and then strain over ice cubes into a Martini glass.
3 Top up with soda.
4 Pour a dash of blackberry liqueur so it floats on the surface of the drink.
5 Top with a few blackberries.

# SLOE GIN

## Ingredients
450 g sloes
225 g caster sugar
1 litre gin

## Method
1 Prick the sloes all over with a fork and put in a jar.
2 Add the sugar and gin to the jar and seal. Shake vigorously.
3 Store in a cool and dark cupboard.
4 Shake the jar every other day for a week.
5 Shake once a week for 2 months.
6 Strain the liquid through a sieve and into bottles.
7 This gin improves with age, so leave for a further 2 months after bottling.

# GLOSSARY

**ALL GRAIN**
Another name for 'full mash'.

**BASE MALT**
In beer, a malt that provides sugar for fermentation.

**CONDITIONING**
The process of carbonating the beer.

**CAMPDEN TABLET**
A sulphur-based product used to kill bacteria.

**CARBOY**
A large fermenting vessel made of glass.

**DEMIJOHN**
A small fermenting vessel made of glass.

**FERMENTER**
A vessel or container in which fermentation takes place. They vary in size and capability.

**FINING AGENT**
A substance used to clarify wine or beer. Examples include Irish moss, bentonite, gelatin and isinglass.

**GRIST**
The name for the combination of crushed grains used in a mash.

**HYDROMETER**
A device used to measure the specific gravity and calculate the strength of alcohol.

**LOVIBOND SCALE**
A scale that measures the depth of colour of a malt.

**MALT**
Malted barley or any other grain that has undergone the malting process.

**MUST**
In wine making, the must is

the liquid resulting from the pulped fruit.

**PITCH**
'Pitching the yeast' means adding the yeast to the wort or must.

**PRIMING**
Adding sugar to aid the carbonation in bottle-conditioned beer.

**RACK**
The process of syphoning off the sediment into a secondary fermenting vessel.

**SEDIMENT**
The dregs of the liquid accumulated at the bottom of the vessel.

**SPARGE**
'Sparging' is the process of rinsing the fermentable sugars from the grains using a fine, continuous spray of hot water.

**SPECIALITY MALT**
Malts used to add flavour and colour, rather than for their fermentable sugars. They are used in small quantities.

**STARCH TEST**
A test to determine if the starch has converted to sugar.

**STEEPING**
Soaking grains in water to release flavour, aroma, body and colour.

**SYPHON**
Tubing needed to 'rack'.

**TANNIN**
Tannin is a phenolic compound in wine which is a natural preservative and contributes a bitter flavour.

**WORT**
In beer, the wort is the liquid that remains after the mashing and boiling processes. The wort contains the sugars that will be fermented after the yeast has been pitched. The word 'wort' is pronounced 'wert'.

# INDEX